MW00943006

1

Bethany **A.** Williams

Live Your Dreams

Bethany A. Williams

Bethany A. Williams

Live Your Dreams

Introduction

Preface: Start Living Your Life Today

Life is an adventure. It is a culmination of people, activities and events that make your experience individual and distinct. **Your life is yours to design and nothing is stopping you from living the incredibly fun-filled and exciting life that you were born to live.**

You can create a life full of adventure. You can achieve life balance. **The journey starts with a dream and ends with making the most of the short life that you have before you.** Are you missing opportunities and adventures all around you? Are you living the best story that you could possibly live? Maybe you've always believed that you could change it; you just aren't sure where to start.

This book will get you started. It is meant to be a motivation to push you off the couch of your life into the life and lifestyle that you enjoy, LOVE, and can't wait for every day. It is meant to wake you up from being a zombie, walking around in mundane existence and activate the dreams and passions in your heart to make the most of the life that you have before you.

It is time to start a new journey that creates for you a satisfying, exciting, and fulfilling life. Redesign your life to create equilibrium. This book will help you dream, plan, and to create an adventure worth living. It will spark ideas and motivate you to design AND LIVE the life that you were created to live.

Bethany A. Williams

Live Your Dreams

Empowering You to Live the Life
You've Always Imagined

Bethany A. Williams

Winning Strategies Book 4

Bethany A. Williams

First edition: January 2013
Second edition: October 2014

For more information or to contact the author visit:
http://www.BethanyAWilliams.com

Blog: http://www.BethanyWilliams.info

Twitter: BethanyAWill

Facebook: LivingtheLifeofYourDreams

YouTube: WinatLifewithBethany

Printed in the United States of America

Live Your Dreams

Dedication

This book is dedicated to my supportive and loving family; Heather & Brian Stirm and Madison, my daughter, son-in-law, and granddaughter, Brandon Williams, my son, and Caleb Williams, my youngest son.

They provide me overwhelming support and love and enable me to live my dreams. They graciously work around my schedule, travel with me, sit at tables and sell books for me, create flyers, and fulfill endless amounts of tasks and activities. For them I'm forever indebted.

I'm thankful for my amazing editor and publicist, Amy VanVleck. Without her, I wouldn't be able to so adequately get a clear and concise message across. She is a huge blessing in my life.

Many thanks to my parents Jim and Elois Eastman for their continued love and support.

Most of all, I'm indebted to my adoring fans that continue to log onto my web site, buy the books, and attend my speeches. I am humbled by the global audience that reads my work and writes in to encourage me. Thank you! You provide more encouragement to me than you will ever know.

Without all of you, I wouldn't be living my dreams.

Sincerely,

Bethany A Williams

Table of Contents

Prologue **10**

Chapter 1 Dare to Dream **12**
Are You Where You Want to Be?
The Journey Takes Time
What about the 'Things'?
Partial Life Success
Shake Free of the Fear
It Starts with a Dream

Chapter 2 Designing the Lifestyle of Your Dreams **32**
Where Are You, Exactly?
Lifestyle Transformation
You Really Can Create Your Own Reality
Plan Your Way into a Better Life
The Steps
Annual Life Planning Process
Peaceful & Quiet Retreat

Chapter 3 Live the Life You're Dreaming Of **48**
The Moment is Now
Distractions
Lifetastic Moments
Believing

Chapter 4 Building the Dream **58**
Iterative Design
Disappointment
Building Rome

Chapter 5 Making it Happen **66**
Making the Plan
Action List

Live Your Dreams

Chapter 6 What's Holding You Back? **76**
The Chains that Bind You
The Quick Action Plan
Success to Catapult you Forward
Go Ahead - Spend the Time, Energy & Money
Experiencing Failure
Dream a Better Dream

Chapter 7 Pinpointing the Action Steps **86**
Action Steps
Schedule Your Life Away

Chapter 8: Celebrating Accomplishments **92**
Everything You Need
Perspective

Chapter 9 The New 'Go'! **98**
Life's Phases
The Fear of the Unknown
Finding a New Start

Chapter 10: Picturing the End Result **106**
Picturing More Time with the Kids
Go For It
Never Give Up

Chapter 11 Making it Work & Staying Focused **115**
The Balls Will Fall

Chapter 12 Living the Dream **117**
The Greater Plan
Life is a Gift
The Travel Journey

Action Plan for Living Your Dream Life **128**

Connecting with the author : **131**
See Bethany's other Winning Strategies series books: 132

Prologue

I was inspired to write this book because of the experiences that I've lived through. I could have been stuck at any number of places in my life. I am just like you, although it may not seem that way from the way that my life is today.

At 18, I was told by my guidance counselor that I was "the stupidest girl that she had ever met" because I would not accept a job at General Motors and choose a life in Flint Michigan. She believed that the job offer that I had at the time was the best future available for me. I was Salutatorian in my high school class, yet she saw the General Motors job and a life in Flint as my best chance at a great future. I didn't dream that for my life. I didn't want to live in Flint or work at GM. I chose a different path. I moved to San Diego and chose to start a life there.

I was deserted by my husband when I was 22. I had a small child and was left to raise that child by myself. I couldn't afford the bills, and often, I was left with less than twenty dollars a week to feed both of us. Those were hard times. There were many days that I thought I would not survive, but I did. I chronicle that journey in the book Winning Strategies for Women.

I couldn't afford to live in California, so I chose to move to Texas to raise my family. It would enable me a better cost of living and a better lifestyle. It would allow me to save for the kid's colleges. I didn't accept that I was trapped.

I live with a debilitating medical condition, severe scoliosis. I have had three major back surgeries and have three artificial discs and steel in my spine. They repositioned my center of gravity in 2004 and I had to learn

Live Your Dreams

to walk all over again. I was told early on that I should never have children, yet I had three. I dreamed up a different life and still choose to do the things I enjoy, like hiking Machu Picchu, climbing to the top of Otumanu in Bora Bora, and many other adventures along the way.

Many of you will read this book and say that "she may be able to dream a better life for herself, but I cannot". You can. You can overcome the obstacles in your life as I have attempted to do. You can dream a better future for yourself and map out a new path. You can get closer to the life that you want to live.

My first husband died six years after he left me alone to raise my daughter. I was embarrassed that he had left me, and I rarely tell that part of my story. To me, I was widowed, and I leave the desertion part of the story far behind in my mind and spirit. I had a failed second marriage, and have lived through untold relationship hardships. I understand loneliness. I understand grief. I understand frustration and a life that seems to not be going your way. I understand what it is like to be overweight, and unhappy with your appearance. Each of these things in your life can change. You can map out a path to a new day and a plan for a better future. You control the path and the journey.

I don't want you to read this book and feel like nothing in your life can be better than it is today. I am just like you. Maybe my path was harder, maybe yours is harder. I have tried to not let my disappointments define me. I made a new plan and remolded my life into more of what I wanted it to be. I continue on a daily journey to live my dreams. Why don't you join me on the journey?

Chapter 1 Dare to Dream

"If you can dream it, you can achieve it."
Zig Ziglar
Motivational Speaker, Author &
Top Salesman

I'm sitting in 9B on an American Airlines flight flying from Dallas to Miami. I'm 30,000 feet in the air, thinking of my international flight to Lima. I'm heading toward Cusco on an ultimate destination of seeing one of the new Seven Wonders of the World.

Machu Picchu, the greatest discovery of Inca ruins ever discovered, is nestled among the Andes Mountains of Peru. It is a destination I've longed to see my entire life. It's a once-in–a-lifetime destination and a once-in-a-lifetime vacation. After Machu Picchu, I'll fly to the Galapagos Islands and walk through nature on a nature discovery that would rival a scene from a National Geographic video or television show.

I'm experiencing anticipation and exhilaration as I imagine what it will be like to walk on the mountaintop and view the world-famous ruins high atop the mountains of the Andes, and walk on the volcanic islands of the Galapagos amongst the unique animals found nowhere else in the world.

So, how did I catapult from a position in life where I'd never traveled, had never left the town I'd grown up in, Flint, Michigan, and certainly had not traveled the globe? The answer is simple; I designed and planned the life I wanted to live. I discovered an amazing reality. You can

Live Your Dreams

live the life you're dreaming of. *You can design the life you want to live.* You can point yourself in the direction that leads you toward the components that you want in your life and the life you want to live. It is amazingly hard to believe. But it has been proved out in both my life and the lives of countless others that I've coached, talked to, and watched as they traveled on their life journeys.

Maybe your life was put on autopilot post high school and college. You may have fallen into a job or role and quit life planning early in your life. Or, you may be at the beginning of the plan and not sure where to take it from here. The journey begins today. You are Frodo at the beginning of an amazing adventure.

Planning it seems, for many of you, is more about whom you will/would marry and how many kids you will/would have or about what job you will/would accept. Your mind doesn't always go that additional step toward what kind of life you want to live.

Some decisions plant you places and you feel stuck. You make one decision that leads to another and so on. But, you are never truly stuck. You simply get into a position where selling all you own and picking up and moving or changing jobs or circumstances becomes scary; it is a risk that you don't consider taking. Change is uncomfortable. It is different from all you know and that difference scares you away from risking anything, daring to live, and daring to follow even the tiniest of your dreams. The journey starts with a dream and ends with making the most of the short life that you have before you.

Are You Where You Want to Be?

Many of you are not where you want to be – for an assortment of reasons: health issues, personal relationship failures, jobs that you've landed in that don't fulfill you, educational aspirations that you may not have finished, and the lists go on. You may be unhappy with the way you look; maybe because you've let yourself go, or given up on yourself to raise kids. Now the kids are gone and you've not gotten back to taking care of yourself. Maybe you wanted to have children and didn't or didn't want to have children and did. At so many points in my life, I found myself right here, unhappy with where I was in life. I didn't want to be a single mom. I hated being broke and disliked my inability to pay my everyday bills.

Wherever your starting point is, this mission is about moving your life closer to the life you want to lead. You cannot give up mid-race and accept that you've lost or not placed well. At any point of the race, you can re-engage. You can start running again from any point in the journey. The journey isn't over til you've drawn your last breath.

You get overwhelmed. You get so far off course, that righting of the ship seems impossible. It is a struggle for you to see any progression, let alone the other side of the track. I so vividly remember that point. As if it happened overnight, I woke up one day caught in an unhappy relationship, in a size 16 body, and an international travelling job that was eating away at every fabric of my life. I didn't have time to make major shifts and changes, but I could slowly invoke a plan that would move me closer to my 'dream' life, the one I imagined. I felt old, I felt fat, and I was discontent and unhappy. I was only 30 years old.

Live Your Dreams

I had stopped thinking about what I wanted out of life years before, and I had begun to go through the motions. I was in survival mode; food on the table, provide for the kids, get to work and home zombie mode.

> *Think about your gifts, talents, and passions*
> *as you begin to consider the life that you want to*
> *lead.*   *Bethany Williams*

You make yourself at home in the graveyards of your buried hopes and dreams. You give up trying because trying was too hard, and it wasn't getting you where you wanted to go. You don't always think about your purpose, and you become caught in a spider web of reality. It pushes you far away from what seems lofty and unattainable and you give up on the search. It is often subconscious. You didn't necessarily wake up one day and say, "I'm giving up on living the life I've always dreamed of. From this point forward, I am determined to live in mediocrity and unhappiness. I will walk through this life as if I'm a zombie." No, it isn't that blatant. If it were, it would be easier for you to recognize. You fall into it like falling down a waterslide in super slow motion.

The Journey Takes Time

A life-altering journey takes time. I am writing this book fifteen years after my realization that my life wasn't what I wanted it to be. In a world of instant microwave meals and spray tans, you are unaccustomed to gradual improvement. Move as fast as you'd like through the journey, but in truth, you have a lifetime to perfect living the life you've always dreamed. Your goal is to start running; not rush to finish the race. Meaning: your life change can be gradual.

My hope is that, as a first step, you will finish this book and through divine intervention and pure will, you will set a course for your life that provides you a plan to use your God-given talents in a fulfilling and satisfying way, moving yourself closer to a life that you will love living.

> *Forget life coaches, I think we should have life conductors. I believe that we need to be guided through the tempo of life, making sure that we are staying in tune and playing to the notes that should be our life.*　　　　*Bethany Williams*

What if it is really possible and you don't give it a chance? What if your doubt and misbelief hold you in the status quo preventing you from living the life you have always dreamed? What if a total transformation is completely possible? Are you willing to risk not trying it? Read on.

What about the 'Things'?

Living the life you are dreaming of isn't about collecting the most things. Oftentimes those things can be what is taking away from your life, trapping you into a life of bills and stress to maintain 'the things.' Maybe you'll arrive at your dream life by selling the horrid assortment of superfluous things that have cluttered up your life and begin living a simpler life, opening up your finances to enjoy things that you really want to do, like travel or quit your job altogether and live in another country for a year.

Live Your Dreams

If you are working long, tedious hours to pay for your passion of scuba diving around the world, maybe your dream life is working in a scuba shop on an island and scuba diving every week, while living a stress-free life in the process.

In the beginning phases of the dreaming process, you are going to simply write down your passions and your dreams. You will scribble down the things that you love to do and the areas that you've found yourself to be gifted in. Therein you will find hints toward the life you were born to live. These will continue to map your course long after you've read this book or decided to live the life you want to lead.

One hundred percent of the people I've talked to that aren't satisfied with their life have never thought about mapping out and taking an alternate path. They feel 'stuck' in the one they have. They think that their dreams are about owning things and not about passions, gifts and talents and their purpose. It is true that finding what you are great at and following your passions toward what you were born to do will often result in more financial success, but it is not about the pursuit of things.

Partial Life Success

We often do better at diving into work or spending all our time on our kids and ignoring our relationships and ourselves. Whatever area you've lost track of in your life, it is never too late to do an assessment and reprogram the path going forward. You design your schedules at work, why can't you dream up a personal life that you want to live? I meet people every day that have achieved tremendous success in one area of their life leaving all other areas barren and deserted. It is doubtful that you are living the life of your dreams if you are pouring all your energy into work and sacrificing most aspects of your personal life.

I used to dream of being a CEO. It was my career path for much of my career. It was my career path. I'd never focused on the lifestyle and schedule perspective; I had assessed my strengths and passions and believed it to be a great career path for me. The closer I got to achieve my goal, I began to assess and recognize the lifestyle and family sacrifices that the majority of CEOs make in order to accomplish that work goal.

I stepped away from that career path in pursuit of a lifestyle of 'of my dreams.' I wanted to have a fulfilling career yet I wanted to be present for my kids and spouse. I wanted to be able to write books and speak to motivate others toward success. I realized that the metaphorical 'life of your dreams' has several facets and, in my dreams, work was only a small piece. I had to save room for hobbies, family, health and fitness and the other priorities that together would form my fulfilling life. I had to make room in my life to build my entire dream picture, not just a component of it.

You too will look at all the facets and create a life that, when the puzzle pieces come together, complete the picture you want to create; and, while doing that, you fulfill your life's purpose, fulfilling your passions and completing your life mission.

Live Your Dreams

Shake Free of the Fear

Fear immobilizes you. It keeps you where you are, doing what you are doing and accepting the life you have. It is easier to do what you have always done and continue down the path that you are on. Any deviation from the path that you are enclosed-in seems, to you, like you are dangling from a broken cable car.

"Eighty percent of what we fear doesn't happen." That statistic always amazes me. I feel a little cheated. Add up in your mind all the time and energy that you have spent worrying about things that never happened.

> *We let the noise of the world drown out the whispers of our hearts.*   *Bethany Williams*

You worry incessantly about unknowns that rarely occur. Your mind creates visions of the worst that can happen, and you stay stuck in the 'what if' analysis paralysis. I have sat at many bedsides of people in the last few years, or moments, of their lives. I am continually amazed that most of their regrets are about the things in life that they didn't try: places they didn't move to, jobs they didn't take, loves that they didn't chase after. Rarely do I ever hear them talk about regrets about what they did do in life.

They wonder what it would have been like to take that assignment overseas, or to marry that woman that they were in love with, or move across country for a job. Fear kept them from moving forward. It stopped them from making a move, wherever that move would have landed them. It kept them from living a dream, following their passions and taking steps to achieve what they often felt were lofty and unachievable dreams.

Mediocrity is our own worst enemy. If life is good, but not exactly what we have dreamed of, we seem to settle in and let it be. If it is horrendous, sometimes we find the strength to make drastic changes to catapult ourselves to a new level. Are you stuck in the middle? Are you living in black and white while dreaming of a color-filled life? It is time to add a little color to the palette of your life.

It Starts with a Dream

So, where does it start? Where do we start designing the life we've always dreamed of living? We dare to dream.

I remember daydreaming in school; it was hard to pay attention to the teacher because I had great daydreams. I daydreamed of marrying a prince, living in a castle, and traveling the world. It is funny what we dream about when we are little children. Somewhere around life's path, we stop dreaming. We find reality and we stop believing that the sky is the limit. We see limits to life and we start morphing our life into a new reality, one that doesn't involve far out dreaming and limitless possibilities.

In order to design the life that you are dreaming of, let yourself dream. Allow your mind to show you the things that captivate you. You were born with a purpose in life and you will be drawn naturally toward that purpose. Do you find yourself energized after doing something? Do you feel excited when you get to do certain tasks or activities? You were made for something. You will feel a magnetic pull toward activities that are your 'gifts.' When you use

Live Your Dreams

your God-given strengths, you will feel fulfilled, energized, and content.

We feel guilty dreaming. It isn't productive. We've been taught to 'get things done' and 'tend to our responsibilities.' We even teach our children to stop dreaming and start making a living. Dreaming becomes foreign to us. It feels like something that we shouldn't be doing. So, go against the conventional, and start dreaming again.

I believe that a seed is planted in each of you. If you do not water that seed and let it grow, you become discontent with life and all that is in it. Finding the gifts buried inside of you and exploring areas that you are magnetically drawn to will move you toward designing the life of your dreams.

So, how do you start? Think back to when you were a kid. What did you dream of as a kid or a young adult? Start writing things down, abstract thoughts and phrases...house in the country, cows, penthouse in the city, two kids, living abroad, painting, playing an instrument, or singing. Whatever comes to your mind, write it down. Start a dreaming journal. It won't make sense at first. It will hold abstract and random thoughts. Turn the page each time you write in it, writing down new thoughts. Don't review the ones previously written until you've been at this for a period of time.

Create your "dream journal" when you are not tired, worn out, stressed or overworked. It will require a few days off, some alone time and some thinking time. It may require a walk in nature or a break from your routine. It may require silence. It may require music. Get away from your normal routine and stretch your mind to a new realm.

Think about fulfilling the desires of your heart.
Bethany Williams

Let your mind wander in several areas of your life. Think about the design that you'd create for the following areas of your life. Today, start a dream journal with a page for each category.

1. Relationships and friendships,
2. Hobbies and special interests,
3. Home Life,
4. Job/Career,
5. Spiritual life and mental peace,
6. and Fitness and health

These six areas form the basis for your dreaming categories. Look at each of the 6 areas and dream a picture of what you'd want for each one.

Action Step: Start a dream journal

Live Your Dreams

Life Dreaming Area 1: Relationships & Friendships

Start a page called 'Relationships' and start by dreaming about relationships. What do you want this area of your life to look like? What would your relationships be like if they were just the way you wanted them to be? Write down random words that come to mind. Define adjectives on this page that describe your desires in this area. Write down your thoughts and dreams. Be open and honest with yourself. Boldly create a dream page that describes your desires for the relationships in your life. What would success look like in this area of your life?

Write down examples of fulfilling relationships in your past that you hold in high esteem. What would you have to do to recreate those types of relationships? Would you have to dedicate time? What would that time look like? With what type of frequency, and what kind of events, would you participate in to recreate these relationships?

Create some action items that match to fulfilling those goals. Potential action items could be: a monthly date night with your husband, a monthly girls night, a weekly one-on-one time with your kiddos, family dinner night, game night, join a dating service, finally accept that blind date, schedule a lunch with X or Y from a past employer, etc. Jot down some goals you'd like to achieve in this area.

Life Dreaming Area 2: Hobbies, Passions & Interests

Have you completely abandoned your hobbies, passions and interests? If you have none, what would they be if you were living the life of your dreams? Write down your visions. Capture your childhood dreams on paper. Write down ideas. Draw out a vision for what it could be. Create potential action items that begin to fulfill those dreams.

Nothing is crazy, and nothing is ridiculous. This is an area that you must leave all your mom's advice behind. It is okay to be 45 and have a hobby of stamp collecting, coin collecting, baseball cards, doll collecting, writing poetry,

Live Your Dreams

etc. Nothing is out of bounds. Do you miss reading books, painting, golfing, or walking by the lake. Find what interests you and write it down. It is a crucial piece to your dream journal. It is a crucial part of living the life you've always dreamed of. Awaken the sleeping passions inside of you.

You will be drawn like a magnet to the area that is your purpose. You will feel the draw, if, and only if, you can open yourself up to the passions that you were born to discover. We get busy and we get stuck in a routine. We let the noise of the world drown out the whispers of our hearts. It will take focus and an effort to awaken your sleeping passions and find an interest that you enjoy burying yourself in from time to time.

Make an action plan that incorporates activities that allow you to try a variety of hobbies on for size. Attend a painting class, go to a musical, buy a paintbrush, buy a travel video, attend a live sporting event, take a photography class, or any other area that strikes an interest in you.

Take time to sample some hobbies and see what sticks.

If travel is a hobby you'd like to explore, than fill that in on your hobby page. If it interests you, dream of places in the world that you'd like to visit and things that you'd like to see.

Whatever hobby you decide that you love will be a great cure for life's doldrums. When work, kids, bills, and the monotony of life sends you into the doldrums, begin thinking about the hobby or special interest that you love to do. Dream up the next time you can spend time on that hobby, trip, experience, or adventure.

The exercise will be fun and refreshing. Watch a travel video, or a show about your hobby, or read about an adventure that you would like to take. Plan to start your hobbies by running through the ideas and possibilities in your mind.

Life Dreaming Area 3: A Home Life Worth Dreaming Of

What does your home life look like in your dreams? Do you have a picture in mind? Write it down. Dream away. Draw a picture of your vision. What characteristics does it have? Write adjectives that describe the home life you are dreaming of. What would it take to get you there? How could you move slowly toward your vision?

We often carry forward expectations of our home life from our childhood or from our childhood dreams. We sometimes don't even realize that we subconsciously are dreaming of a certain picture or expectation. Allow yourself to fill it out in your dream journal. Explore your inner self and document your vision. Dream a dream of the home life you dream of.

We get so caught up in life in all the other areas that we lose track of this one. We forget about the important things in life and focus our attention on the job and other areas, leaving our home life out of dreams and not getting the focus or attention that it needs.

Live Your Dreams

What adjectives come to mind? Job them down. Paint a word picture or cut out pictures of things that you'd like to have in your home life. You may just write down some words that you'd like to incorporate into your home life; spontaneous, peaceful, experiencing great food, adult kids that visit often, feeling loved, being cared for, experiencing intimacy, and a happier marriage. Write down your desires. Put them on paper. Begin to dream up the perfect family/home life for you.

Plot out some action steps. It is exciting to start walking in the direction of your dreams. You control the path and destiny. Begin to create a plan that gets you where you want to be.

Life Dreaming Area 4: Working Toward a Career You Love

You noticed that work wasn't first on the list. For many of you, that is where your mind wanders first. You do not live to work, or at least you shouldn't. You work to live. What does the career of your dreams look like? If you are early in your life journey, what careers interest you? What sectors of the industry do you find interesting? If you are already in a career/job, do you love it? If not, what do you *like* about it? What do you dislike about it?

What does the career/job of your dreams look like? Write down your thoughts in your dream journal. Create a few action items that you can schedule to start yourself on your new journey. Potential ideas that you follow up on include: updating your LinkedIn profile, updating your resume, searching online career postings for job listings that sound fun, reaching out to past co-workers, scheduling some networking events, etc. If you don't have a job, set regular goals to search out and find the job of your dreams.

Dreams start with a thought. You can then scribble those thoughts down in your dream journal. Once you formulate the vision, you can begin plotting out action items to move you down the path closer to your dreams.

Sometimes we give up before we set a course. Start dreaming, set out a course, and plot your action items to move you slowly toward your vision. A trip is achieved by setting a course and slowly walking in the direction of the goal.

Life Dreaming Area 5: Spiritual Life & Mental Peace

We often leave our spiritual health behind, but it is a vital area of our life. What does your spiritual life and mental well-being look like in your dreams? Think about the goals that would match to that. Write down action items that match the spiritual life you'd like to have. Write down some potential action items, such as: attending a church service regularly, having a daily devotional, taking a mission trip to another country, purposeful quiet time once a day, etc.

In order to live the life you're dreaming of, each area of your life needs a dream and focused attention. To be in harmony, your life needs relational elements, an intact relationship with God, time to focus on your passions, and family focus.

Live Your Dreams

Life Dreaming Area 6: Amazing Fitness & Health

Next, dream about health and fitness goals that would get you to the physical size and shape and health status that you long for.

If you were dreaming about the 'fitness and health' aspect of your life, what would it look like? What does the body, or health, 'of your dreams' look like? Think of goals that match to your dreams. Write them in your dream journal.

Write it down in your dream journal. Think of goals that match to your dreams. Cut out a picture that depicts a desired end goal for your body and your appearance. Think about physical activities that you enjoy. Where we normally go wrong on fitness and health goals is that we try a one size fits all program. You are unique. You will enjoy differing physical activities than potentially others around you. Think of unconventional ideas for keeping fit, at least the ones not normally covered in health and fitness magazines. Consider activities like the batting cages, hiking, walking around the mall, tennis, golf, jujitsu, boxing, mountain climbing, biking, pilates, or yoga.

List a few physical activities that you enjoyed doing long ago. How did you keep in shape as a teenager? Maybe you have never felt physical energy or never been in shape, but always wanted to. It doesn't matter if you want to try to jazz dancing, it is about identifying the ways that you either enjoyed staying in shape in the past, or think you may enjoy doing today. Dream up a good idea of activities, and desired health status for you if you could live the way you've always dreamed of living.

If you had all the time in the world, would you eat better? Have you considered what you would eat if you could change your diet? Are there healthy foods you enjoy eating?

Think of potential action items that could aid you on your journey. Potential action items could be: heart smart healthy eating, buy a pair of tennis shoes, walk to the corner once a day, decide to take the stairs in your office building, begin exercising once a month, sign up for a yoga class, go to the batting cages, buy a blender to make healthy shakes, lose 5 pounds in the next 3 months, watch Hungry for Change, Food Inc, or Super Size Me to move you toward healthier eating, etc. Find easy, small steps to get you started on the path.

Accept that you do create your destiny. You create the direction that you are driving your life. You are in control. Preparing a plan can get you where you want to go.

Live Your Dreams

Write down your dreams in each of these areas. Create the biggest, craziest, and most audacious goals and dreams that you can come up with. Shoot high and make them as sky high as you can. I had several BHAG goals when I started my journey. I still have a long list of goals that I am working to attain.

Bethany's Big Goals:
- I would like to reach a point of financial success that would allow me live a certain lifestyle and schedule without having to worry about meeting basic financial obligations. I'd like to have a passive revenue stream that maintains the lifestyle that I enjoy living.
- One of my big goals was to become a professional speaker. I have achieved that goal and I immensely enjoy speaking at events. Now my goals are focused on keynote addresses and the frequency and locations that I speak. I would enjoy more international speaking gigs.
- I would love to have my own radio show, talk show, or travel show. I am still working on this goal.
- I want to remain in tip top shape and keep a healthy lifestyle (would love to look years younger than I am).
- I would like to write one book a year.
- I want to see the world and wish to continue to travel to remote and intriguing locales annually. I would love living on a beach in an exotic location for a year.

The journey all starts with your dreams. Awaken the child inside of you and start dreaming again. Begin your journey by dreaming a dream for your life. Start the process by forming the vision.

Chapter 2 Designing the Lifestyle and Life of Your Dreams

"Delight yourself in the LORD and he will give you the desires of your heart."

Psalm 37:4

When I selected a career, plotted out my college courses and began a life direction, I didn't think at all about lifestyle design. I didn't think about the kind of life I wanted to live. I wasn't thinking about the desires of my heart.   I was thinking about survival. Since survival was my focus, I didn't focus on the life I wanted to live. I focused on 'getting by.'

My focus was on eating and a roof over my head. I hadn't thought through varying questions to place me in the life and career that I was destined to live, the one I'd dreamed of, or the one I was most gifted for. I never considered for a moment that it was even a possibility. Each of you has been born with a purpose. Often times our school systems and universities don't accurately prepare us for our purpose, our destiny, or for creating and living the life of our dreams.

There are great questions that you can ask yourself early on or as you consider alternate occupations and fields:

- Would you prefer a job where you work inside or outside?
- What climates do you enjoy? What about seasons?
- Are you a people person or would you prefer a job in a back room?

Live Your Dreams

- Do you like to organize things? Or do you prefer chaos?
- Do you like structure, or environments without structure?
- Are you always prompt or usually late?
- Do you dream of owning your own business?
- What subjects are you drawn to?
- What tasks/activities do you enjoy?
- What fields hold your interest?

There are hundreds of questions that you can think through as you design the life you want to live, many of which you may have missed contemplating or considering.

If you explore the elements that you would like to incorporate into your life, stepping toward those will bend the path that you are on, ultimately ensuring that you arrive closer to your desired destination. You can design the life you want to live and then move in that direction, moving closer to living the life of your dreams.

Where Are You, Exactly?

Often we are too discouraged to assess our location and current circumstances, because by doing so, we admit to where we are today. By assessing our current G.P.S. in life, we admit to ourselves that we are not where we want to be. Our current location may equate to somewhere that we'd rather *not* be. It may seem so many miles away from where we want to be that we cannot visualize getting there. This will require a little faith.

In order to map out exactly where you'd like to be on your trip, you must assess the starting location. In Chapter 1 you considered dreams, wants, and action items that you wanted as components of your dream life. Now you must review your dream journal and decide your starting points for the journey.

Where are you today? What areas need the most work and in what areas are you already somewhat embarking on? Is it the direction that you want to go?

Draw six lines on a sheet of paper to represent the six areas that encompass your life: relationships/friends, fitness & health, spiritual & mental peace, hobbies/passions & interests, work life, and your family/home life. Plot a point on each line to determine where you feel you are today. A point all the way to the left means 'not content,' and a point all the way to the right is 'in the perfect place/content.' A point in the middle is average satisfaction.

If assigning a letter grade is easier, then grade each area with an A, B, C, D, or N for 'not at all' where you want to be. There are no failing grades. You are either right where you want to be, right on target in some areas, in need of some improvement, or in need of a change. The journey is easier once you've realized which areas aren't where you want them to be and then you can work on them. It is a realization that a journey is required. It may not be required in each area.

You do not have to tackle them all at once. This is your assessment. In business, we create business plans that attack the weakest areas first. In your personal life, you

Live Your Dreams

determine which areas you'd like to prioritize, and in what order. It's *your* life.

In my personal assessment several years ago, I had a journey in each of the six areas. It was this assessment that started my journey toward the life I'm living today. It was the starting point to creating the life that was closer to the one I was dreaming of. Your assessment of your current positioning will help you to set your trajectory. You can map out your path and journey from the starting point. I've had the honor of witnessing hundreds of people plot their current location, map out a trajectory, and set themself off on a journey to discover a new reality. It is beautiful to watch.

The journey of life is going to move past you faster than you've ever thought possible. It will catapult you forward and, before you know it, much of your life will be behind you. Think of your journey as short, and plan for taking advantage of every minute you've been given. Thinking that life is long only leads us to a life of procrastination. We continually put off things that we should do today, anticipating a tomorrow that may never come.

Lifestyle Transformation

A component of living your dream life is about having the lifestyle that you want to have, or at least one closer to the one you've dreamed of. If you can focus on the lifestyle you desire, and not just about the job you want or the field you'd like to be in, you will achieve a closer match to the life of your dreams.

We are focused. Our minds are wrapped around our career goals and we jump into work full force. We work hard and attain a career path that is moving us up the ladder. We concentrate on the job we want and we work to attain it.

Living a life that is full and rich, and closer to the life you've always dreamed of isn't just about the job you want, it is about the lifestyle you want. You are achieving what you set out to achieve, but have you set the right targets?

It could be time for a lifestyle redesign. Our career goals, if done well, are only part of our strategy. Fully rounding out our life entails a picture that includes health goals, food and nutrition goals, vacation and personal life goals, family goals, and the spiritual goals mapped out in Chapter 1.

To be all that you can be, you will need to devote time, attention, and energy into creating a lifestyle that you will love and enjoy living. It may mean that you choose a different career, one that affords you more time at home or more time for a passion, hobby or love interest.

This lifestyle redesign is about creating equilibrium. It is about life balance to a whole new level. It is about attaining more than just career success or just family success. It is about achieving life, family, joy, and personal fulfillment success. It is about living life on a whole new level.

I stepped off of a CEO track when I assessed my current plot points. Becoming a CEO would help me attain financial goals, but it would sacrifice (in my personal assessment) the home life and equilibrium with hobbies and civic organizations that I wanted to ultimately achieve. It was a lifestyle choice. I put together a plan that would

Live Your Dreams

create a lifestyle and a life of my dreams. The combination of all of the components, working in unison, could help me to attain the life I of my dreams.

Prior to stepping off the CEO track, my work life consumed every facet of my life. I didn't have time for vacations, or enough time for my family. I couldn't volunteer time or energy anywhere, because I was left with no energy after the day job. It overwhelmed me. Hobbies were a far distant dream that were completely out of reach. I didn't have time to write, blog, mentor others, speak, or do much of anything that I love to do.

As you consider the life you want to lead, rethink the components of your life giving each a weighted influence. Don't ignore one area of your life to focus completely on another. Life isn't just about the job you want, it is about the lifestyle you desire. You can create a lifestyle that is closer to what you would like it to be. You are driving your career and your life. Drive in the direction that you'd like to go.

You Really Can Create Your Own Reality

At this point, you are probably wondering, can you really create your own reality? Well, you definitely can. You can create a life closer to the life you've always dreamed of. The answer is a combination of a few actionable steps that this book will walk you through:

- Dream a Dream – Chapter 1
- Sketch Out the Plan - Chapter 2
- Pinpoint the Steps – Chapter 7
- Affirm Your Accomplishments- Chapter 8

- Picture the End Result and Act Accordingly- Chapter 10
- Stay Focused – Chapter 11

We get overwhelmed because we live in a society that constantly bombards us with instant gratification and fast results. True metamorphosis is a gradual process that entails time. You need to become a believer. Make yourself a believer in you and your abilities to transform your life into what you'd like it to be.

> *I want to wake you up and move you toward living the life that you want to live. I want to help you fight the biggest enemy in your journey that you face: yourself.*
> *Bethany Williams*

It took me more than four years to transform my position at the hospital into a leadership role. It took me five years to build my personal brand, move into broad-scale mentoring capabilities, get an audience for my motivational blog, and write two books. Make a plan to achieve slow and steady progress in your goals. As you move toward them, it will seem like you've accomplished so much so fast to you and others around you. Over time, it will be hard for you to recall what it was like before the transformation.

It is time for you to transform your world. It is time to create a new reality. It is time to wake you up and move toward living the life that you want to live. Now you must fight the biggest enemy in your journey that you face- yourself. Find the confidence to start the journey. It will take a daring spirit with perseverance to succeed. You can do it. Let's start with a plan.

Live Your Dreams

Plan Your Way into a Better Life

We all spend a significant amount of our time planning: planning our day, planning a project at work, planning resolution for a dispute at the office, planning our chores and yard work, and a myriad of other things. How much time do we spend planning our life?

Why do you think we spend so-o-o-o-o much time focused on things that, for the most part, would not rank very high on our priority list? I think that they are necessary things to keep our job, keep groceries in the cupboards, keep the car running, etc. They are plans that jump up in front of us and we are forced to act on them without forethought or consideration. We don't have a choice. We run through life in rote motion. Like zombies, we walk through life in a daze. We are not really living each moment; we simply go through the motions and let life move us in its own direction.

Doesn't it make sense that on occasion we should be planning our lives? On occasion we should be writing down the things that move us, motivate us, and cause a spark in us.

We should be making a plan for the life we want to lead. You really don't think it 'just happens' without a plan, do you?

It is never too late to start a life-planning process. This plan has sections for desired accomplishments, personal goals, family goals, health goals, work goals, vacations you'd like to take, educational/learning interests, and civic or community efforts that interest you. This plan forms the basis for where you funnel some of your free time and resources over the years.

As you move through the stages of your life, you will have more or less time to devote to certain areas of your life. As life ebbs and flows, you will be able to focus more or less in certain areas. If you don't consciously decide on your focus, life will rush in and decide your focus for you. You will open your eyes to discover that you are at the end of the path and you have little time left and you have not accomplished your life's goals. Don't let that happen.

Live Your Dreams

In lieu of no plan, life forms a plan of its own. If you are not planning, the life you are living is just happening and is not waiting for you to plan. You are not avoiding a homework assignment by not planning; rather, you are avoiding a full and rich life that encompasses some of the hopes and dreams that you are yearning for.

> *If you don't consciously decide on your*
> *focus, life will rush in and decide on your*
> *focus for you.*   *Bethany Williams*

We tend to not plan. We lean toward a life that falls easily in front of us. We walk the path that is laid down before us and lack discipline that would be required to proceed through the planning process. This describes you no longer! Today you are going to begin a simple plan that will set your course. This begins the next step of your journey. The plan you are creating marks a step of action necessary to get where you want to go.

I once presented a speech to a large group of women on the topic of the Life Planning Process. One lady in the audience was well into her sixties. She expressed dismay that she was just now learning about a process that she wished that she had begun forty years earlier. It is never too late to begin a life-planning process. Planning creates the action steps that take you toward your dreams. You can create those steps toward your dreams in any amount of time. Today is a new day and a new opportunity to start the plan.

In each area of your life that you have established a picture of what your desired state would be, you will assign a few action steps to encompass the next few years. There is a tactical progression to achieving a goal. If you are interested in becoming a dental hygienist, the first action step may be to research school options and requirements for admission.

The Steps

Take each area of your life and find two or three tactical action steps that you could take to move yourself closer to the goal. If you've always dreamed of taking a vacation to Paris, then write down a few tactical steps you could take: research trip options and pricing, start a vacation fund, and buy a book on Paris travel. Take the first step in several of your dream areas.

This is not the time to be practical. It is not the time to focus on whether or not you *think* that you have the money. If you haven't done the research yet, you have no facts, so you do not know what is possible.

Make the tactical planning steps easy to achieve. If you want to lose 80 pounds, start with a tactical plan to research gym memberships and take a cooking class on healthy cooking. If you make the steps too hard to achieve, they will keep you from attempting the journey. When I wanted to lose 40 pounds, I made the goals for each month 2-4 pounds. It was easier to achieve smaller goals and each month that I achieved my goal was a positive step toward the longer journey.

You will have more action items for the areas of your life that are furthest away from your desired state. Remember

Live Your Dreams

that you will renew this plan annually, so focus solely on the next 12 months. Segment these action items by month and plot them on your calendar. Pick a day and a time to enter the calendar entries. For the above example, you may decide in 2 weeks that you will research gym memberships on a Saturday at 2PM. Enter the appointment on your paper or electronic calendar or To Do list. I have found a newfound appreciation for Wunderlist.com. It allows me to keep a massive To Do list to track accomplishments toward my journey.

For vacation planning, select a time when you annually find yourself with a few extra hours. Some have found success between Thanksgiving and Christmas. It seems that many have more down time during this time period and it may afford you a little vacation dreaming time. Put it on a Saturday in your Outlook calendar from 2-4 PM or on a Sunday afternoon to 'Research Travel Destinations to ?' I do this and I look forward to these appointments on my calendar.

You can also plot out events that you'd like to attend. If you'd like to attend two professional sporting events, you may put a calendar entry on your calendar for the first week of January to 'Explore professional game schedule and choose two potential games'.

Keep ticking away at each area on your list and choose a couple action items for each area. Plot them on your calendar and set a task list of To Do's to begin your journey. Remember, every step moves you closer to the destination.

Annual Life Planning Process

Each year you will set a plan to review your Life Planning Process. Think of it as your Annual Employee Review only it is much more important. You may only have your current job for a few years, but you will have your life, your family, and your memories forever.

Once a year set aside time to review each area of your life. Look at the graph of where you rated the areas the prior year and review your action steps. Rate the areas again with full attention on the current condition and progression. Assign action items for the next year. For special focus, consider taking a special course or paying special attention to one area that you feel discontent over its current status.

The second time you review your plan, you may feel courageous enough to ask a family member or friend to weigh in. Sometimes we don't see ourselves clearly. We may think that we are doing a fantastic job of balancing our work and family time, yet our spouse or children may disagree. Getting an outside-in perspective may help you validate your plan or alter it accordingly.

If the action steps that you set were not realistic, set more realistic action steps that are attainable this time around. You will be disappointed in yourself if your action steps are

Live Your Dreams

not attainable. The difference between expectations that are too high and a reality that is much lower equals dissatisfaction and depression. Be sure that your goals are attainable and that the action steps are realistic. This is about a slow and steady move toward the life you are destined to live, not about a 900 mile an hour pedal to the medal to end the race. Slow and steady will win the race.

This annual review is often hard to do. We have so many responsibilities that weigh us down and too much on our plates. We want to take time to plan and review but we find ourselves running the kids to and fro, making dinner, doing the laundry or simply falling onto the couch too exhausted to think. Turning on the TV is easier because we don't have to think, and we don't have to face the reality that is our life today.

Peaceful & Quiet Retreat

It is easier to re-evaluate your life plan while away from your house and your normal routine. Consider taking a trip without any distractions. Leave the kids with relatives and step away from it all. It doesn't have to be a costly vacation; it can be a tent on a lake. The goal is to relieve yourself of your everyday responsibilities, and run away from the TV and the household chores long enough to experience silence and be able to hear yourself think. You could be in a bedroom at a friend's house. Find a quiet place to get out of your normal routine and explore your innermost thoughts.

You can use this time to rethink, re-measure, and re-evaluate each component of your life. Think of it like a management retreat or a teambuilding exercise. Companies employ these tactics every year. No matter how great the year before was, companies take their leadership team away from it all and put down the goals for the coming year. They reposition. They rethink the plan. They plan for new goals and aspirations. They set targets and dreams for the company for the next year. This will be the goal of your personal annual planning retreat.

If you work in business, you probably have spent a significant amount of your energy and time planning for business. I'd dare say that it would equate to a significantly greater amount of time and energy than you have ever spent on planning your life. Think on that for a moment. When I came to this realization, it was startling. I had spent years of my life planning success for businesses that I worked for. Yes, I had labored away in planning processes for companies yet, at the time, I had never planned my own success. Now it seems silly, almost preposterous that I would spend years of my life planning company success and never consider creating a success plan for my own life.

Each year I recommit to a plan. I evaluate where I am in each area of my life. One year on such a vacation, I decided that I no longer wanted to work at my current job. It was not giving me a chance to live. My life was work and all aspects of my waking moments were devoted to work. I had developed an unhealthy balance and decided that upon returning from vacation, I would begin looking for a new position. Since I determined my discontent to be high, I decided to spend a significant amount of time once I returned looking for something new.

Live Your Dreams

Annually re-evaluate. Make a plan to move forward. Alter your action steps and create new steps for the following year. Plot your new action steps on your calendar. You will notice a progression from year to year. The increased focus and attention to your life plan will help you to focus on the plan and move the ball forward. Like in business, focus and attention will move you forward.

In business, we print out the goals for the year. We make flyers. We create wallet cards for our employees to carry the goals with them. We post them on our desks and send monthly reminders. Print out your goals. If your goal is to see Paris, print a picture of it and tape your picture on top of it. Post the picture on your desk at work. Visualize success in each area of your life.

I once printed a picture of a red convertible and taped a picture of my head in the driver's seat. It took years before I could buy the car, but I could visualize success and what it would look like years before I actually achieved it. I wrote out a goal that said, if you achieve X promotion resulting in Y increase in salary, you will get your car. I put a big smiley face next to the goal and the reward defined. When I got the promotion, I went out and bought a little red Capri convertible. It was, at the time, a pretty risky expense for a single mom, but I loved it. Picture your success. Create your plan and visualize what success will look like. I still enjoy driving a cute little red convertible.

Create an annual plan to re-assess your progress. Find time in your schedule to make annual plan revisions. You will enjoy these retreats better than any work retreat you have ever been on.

Chapter 3 Go Ahead – Live the Life You're Dreaming Of

"Remember how fleeting is my life."

Psalm 89:47

The Moment is Now

We are missing out. Life is brief. We have but a limited amount of time to live. We are running through life-missing the moments that rush by us- not observing the little details of life and overlooking the most amazing pieces of our lives. We are not living in the moment or even conscious of the limited amount of time that we have been given.

How can you live the life you are dreaming of when you only a spectator of your life today? How often are you 'in another moment' as life is passing by?   It is as if you are in a movie theatre, having paid to attend the movie and you are on your Ipad watching another movie. You are living in one moment and attending another.

In order to live the life of your dreams, you will need to focus on living in this very moment. Begin by focusing on relishing the gifts of relationships, loved ones, and enjoying the present moments in time. Each moment of your life is precious. Work to begin to listen carefully, absorb the air around you and live in each moment that you have been given. Each moment is a gift.

Try to live in the moment today. Have you ever stopped to soak in the moment and take a picture in your mind of the

Live Your Dreams

current place and time in your mind to re-live at a later time?

I talked to people daily. They have ideas of events they'd like to attend. There are places they'd like to go. They know of jobs that they'd like to apply for, and they dream of experiences that they want to do "someday," but they aren't planning any of them today.

Life is our biggest adventure. It is the biggest project you will ever be given. It isn't like cutting the lawn, you cannot just put it off for a time. Unfortunately, the 'grass' of our dreams doesn't grow so tall that we cannot ignore it anymore. Our dreams can go unnoticed and fade into the background of our busy existences. We forget what they were at one time and we stop trying to achieve them as we age.

Planning events and activities that we love to do becomes a chore and we begin to move through life in a trance, doing today what we did yesterday. We fall into a monotonous existence, not living a life of joyful exuberance. We forget how fleeting our life is and we live a life of quiet desperation. We have a song in us that we are not signing.

You were made with a purpose and you may not be living the purpose that you were born to live. God created you with special talents. He knit you together in your mother's womb and there is no time like the present with which to begin the life that you were born to live.

ethany **A. W**illiams

Distractions

Your life is unfolding in the present. Often times, you are letting the present slip by. Time is rushing past you and you don't observe it or notice it. You are wasting precious moments of your lives as you worry about the future and think about the past.

The world around you makes it difficult to focus on the present. Your cell phone beeps, your email dings, your phone rings, and you are constantly peppered with distractions that take you out of the moment. You find yourself always doing something, and you are allowing very little time to practice being still.

When you are on vacation, you worry about the work piling up at the office. When you are at work, you are fantasizing about being on vacation. You aren't aware of your thoughts. Rather, your thoughts control you. "Ordinary thoughts course through our mind like a deafening waterfall," writes Jon Kabat-Zinn, the biomedical scientist who introduced meditation into medicine. In order to feel more in control of your mind and your life, to find the sense of balance that is eluding you, you need to stop the deafening waterfall in your brain, and, as Kabat-Zinn puts it, to "rest in stillness—to stop doing and focus on just being."

Find a way to create a 'live in the moment,'
fabulous lifetastic moments that you will
not only enjoy living, but will cherish for
the rest of your life! ~ *Bethany Williams*

Live Your Dreams

You will need to learn to live in the moment. Living in the moment is the ability to have a focused attention on the present. When you focus on the current moment you are living in, you realize that you are not your thoughts; you become an observer of your thoughts from moment to moment without judging them. You begin to be with your thoughts as they are, neither grabbing at them nor pushing them away. Instead of letting your life go by without living it, you awaken to experience it moment by moment.

If you can achieve this, it can lead to your achieving a happier, more exciting life. It is a key component of living the life you are dreaming of.

Lifetastic Moments

Life planning and enjoyment doesn't have to be apocalyptic, it can be more about daring to see a movie on a Tuesday afternoon or spending a couple hours doing nothing but flipping through a magazine, guilt free. Have you ever thought about creating a lifetastic memory that could entail just a few hours? Some of my most enjoyable memories are events that were scheduled for only 2-4 hours. I'll give you a few examples:

Layover Fun
Once, while traveling with the family, we had to connect in San Francisco. I was cashing in free airline points and it necessitated an out of the way layover that was for five hours. I called around and found a limousine that was available and negotiated a discount rate to rent the limousine for three hours to go see the Golden Gate Bridge, eat at the waterfront, and 'tour' San Francisco.

Who says that a two and a half-hour tour can't be loads of fun? I think you should take whatever time, opportunities and resources you have to innovatively create experiences in life that you can enjoy. We should take every opportunity to 'stop and smell the roses.'

Our first stop was to ride over the Golden Gate Bridge. Stopping at the viewpoint, we tried unsuccessfully to see the Bridge through the intense fog. Even without the full view, the view as we passed under it was exhilarating. We drove down a winding road to the quaint town of Sausalito. It turned out to be an appealing, waterfront town full of little shops and restaurants. I made a mental note that I'd like to return there someday.

We continued our two-hour tour and saw an amazing view of the haunting Alcatraz. Veering back over the bridge we stopped by Fisherman's Warf and tasted fresh crab, oyster stew, fish sticks and shrimp cocktail. It was delicious. I can still remember the taste as I write this.

We jumped back in the car, and sped back to the airport. Our two and a half-hour tour of San Francisco was amazing fun.

We had the best time in those few hours. The whole adventure came in under $300 yet yielded tons of fun. We originally thought we were stuck for a long layover in San Francisco and that it will be horrendous. Then we turned our thoughts toward "what would make this fabulous?"

Take each moment in your life and commit to making it fabulous. You own your path and the destinations. You can

Live Your Dreams

turn awful into fabulous. You can create a lifetastic moment.

Business Jaunt

While in Monterey, California, on a three-day business trip, I noticed that due to flight schedules, my flight the following day was at 11:30 am. I set my alarm for the break of dawn. I bounded out of bed and walked to the coastline.

The sun hadn't yet risen. I spotted seagulls catching their morning breakfast. Sea lions were playfully swimming about, chatting it up and seemingly having a rowdy conversation with each other. The waves were crashing to shore.

As I walked down the beach, the light of day began to peek over the horizon. Light shed over the incredible views and- as in life- as I traveled, the views grew even more beautiful.

My feet sank into the sand and sand oozed through my toes. Waves ran toward me, almost covering me in water up to me knees. I ran away from the waves, laughing like a little child- perfectly content to play alone on the beach in the early morning hours.

I traveled on for miles, entering Cannery Row and spotted a Starbucks. I got excited at the thought of a warm, hot liquid to warm me from the 50ish temperature that surrounded me. I was living in the moment absorbing life and the beauty of nature. I was experiencing the fullness of each moment and creating a memory to last a lifetime.

You can refresh yourself in the shortest amount of time. In

this 3-hour vacation, I experienced a total mind reset. It refreshed my soul. It gave me a new fortitude with which to face the burdens of life.

Create a memory by taking advantage of the opportunities that surround you. You are walking past opportunities to live in the moment every day.

Hiking Adventure
A co-worker was off on maternity leave and she requested that I cover her accounts. I was in sales at the time and needed to fly to Salt Lake City to meet with a client for her.

My meeting ended early, and I couldn't change my flight. I was done by 1 p.m. and my flight wasn't til early the next morning. Only 29 miles from the airport is the famous ski resort called Snowbird. Now, I'm not a skier, and well, it wasn't the right time of the year for snow. I am, however, an avid hiker and nature lover.

I drove to the resort in my rental car and hired a guide to show me the mountain. I hiked to the top of one of the peaks with a mountaineer guide at my side. The views were amazing. When I reached the top, I experience the mountaintop thrill of climbing to the top of any peak. It was exhilarating

I took the trolley down. The guide laughed at me and said that normally people ride the trolley up and hike down.

For those few hours, I wasn't thinking about work or bills, or kid problems. I wasn't thinking about how much money I had in my retirement account, or any other problems that had been on my mind before the hike. I was living in the

Live Your Dreams

moment. I was enjoying God's country and soaking up the moment of my life.

Believing

"And my God will meet all your needs according to his glorious riches in Christ Jesus."

Philippians 4:19

What is holding you back from living the life you are dreaming of? Do you know what your gifts and talents are? Have you stopped to dream a dream of the life that incorporates your skills and talents and allows you to live the life that you were born to live?
Sometimes we don't believe that it is possible. We don't acknowledge that we can live the life we are dreaming of. God has promised us the desires of our hearts and that he will meet our needs. He doesn't want you to live a life of quiet desperation. He doesn't want you to go through life as a zombie, not living a life of joy and not doing the work and exploring the passions that were put in you from the moment you were formed in your mother's stomach.

It is often easier for parents to think about the best lives for your children, than it is for you to dream a better life for yourself. It is hard for us to believe. It is often hard to reawaken the lost dreams of our childhood or acknowledge that being a good mom or dad doesn't mean completely rejecting the passions that we were born with.

You are being pulled toward a passion. You have a magnetic pressure that is pulling you toward hopes and dreams that you have for yourself. If you have tune a deaf ear toward these voices, than you may have become an expert at 'not believing' that your life can be any different than it is today.

I'm asking you to believe. I'm requesting that you risk losing the mundane components of your life to dream a better existence. I'm imploring you to take a chance and reawaken the dreams that were put inside of you since the day you were born. You will feel energized when you do the work that God has called you to do. You will have a cup overflowing with joy. You will experience a satisfying and completely fulfilling life, full of joy and promise. Believe in your destination and the journey ahead of you with the same intensity and fervor that you feel toward the futures of your loved ones or children if you have them. Absorb the energy that you had as a teen and ignite the fire that you once felt toward the world that you were going to conquer and the dreams that were going to be your life.

You've been let down. You've experienced disappointment. As you lived through these experiences, each one chipped away at your resolve. Each one deadened a nerve. Each disappointment moved you further away from believing that anything was ever going to be better or that you were ever going to live the life of your dreams. You got lost in disappointment and you buried the dreams that you feel that you could never achieve.

Get out a shovel. Dig some of them up. It is never too late to begin activating some of those hopes and dreams. Now is the time to fervently seek those components of long buried dreams.

Often, we 'give up' and we live vicariously through others' Facebook posts, blogs, and Twitter activity. We

Live Your Dreams

watch movies and 'go places' through the screen in front of us. We watch people work out on exercise videos, yet we have become sedentary and our lives bland.

Some of you are living in abusive relationships and are convinced that you deserve it. You don't believe there is a way out and you have accepted where you are. Don't accept it any longer. Take the courage to change the path. I know you can. Many of you are working jobs that you hate and you don't believe it can change. It can change. Accept the possibility of an alternate reality. You can start here. You can start now. Start by believing in the possibilities. Believe in yourself.

Years ago, the radio was the only form of mass entertainment. Houses were quiet without ringing phones and bleeping emails, and people dreamed. As kids, we spent hours and hours dreaming. Today, we have filled our heads with too much noise and, in the noise we have lost the ability to believe that anything else is possible. The noise provides a constant static in our heads that keeps us from hearing the whispers of our heart.

We have lost ourselves in all the constant noise and we are no longer able to hear our own thoughts. We are being drowned out by the incessant noise and constant distractions. We have stopped believing in ourselves and we have given up on our belief that we can build a better life. We feel beat down and defeated. Today you will get yourself up and start the journey. You will begin believing in yourself even if you don't feel that you can.

Live Your Dreams

Chapter 4   Building the Dream

"A dream doesn't become reality through magic; it takes sweat, determination and hard work."

Colin Powell
American statesman

Iterative Design

So, how does this transformation start after all the dreaming? What gets us from dream to ready, set, go? It happens with slight changes applied, changes made, then revisions applied. I think of it as iterative design. Product development departments use this in new product development. An example is Apple as they started with their creation of the iPhone. It wasn't fabulous on their first go at it. It progressed with each release. You will apply the same design process and revision review as they did with the iPhone or the iPad or any other invention.
.

Iterative design is defined by www.reference.com as "a design methodology based on a cyclic process of prototyping, testing, analyzing, and refining a work in progress. In iterative design, interaction with the designed system is used as a form of research for informing and evolving a project, as successive versions, or iterations of a design are implemented."

You create a model, test it, analyze it, and continue to refine it. You really don't know if you are 'there' yet until you try it out several times, each time making revisions and improvements to the design. I'm suggesting that you do this with your life. I'm recommending that you make small changes, test them, analyze them, and live with them for a while. Make changes to alter those designs or decisions and continue to evolve the results until you are closer to the goal.

The further you are from the destination that you 'd like to arrive, the more iterations it will require to move you closer to the life you are dreaming of. When we are far away from where we want to be, often times we stop dreaming. Even worse, sometimes we stop trying to reach our goals and dreams altogether. In reality, the distance from the goal is not important, the fact that you are moving closer toward the destination one step at a time is the most important component of living your dreams.

We are more comfortable with instant results. We do not like to wait. Although we are often staring at a long life ahead of us, we aren't patient enough to map out the path and work toward achieving it. If we have forty pounds to lose, losing two pounds a month and taking two years to meet our goal seems incredibly long and so we live with the forty pounds indefinitely. In our unwillingness to take a slow approach, we don't do anything. We rush to the goalpost and don't realize that we've dropped the football. In our impatience to wait for results, we achieve nothing at all.

What if you decided to cut out one small thing from your diet, and that small change caused you to lose two pounds a month. [Hint: this is iterative design.] What if that loss kept up for the next two years? You would lose forty-eight pounds after two years. Iterative design is about mapping out changes and slowly evolving your life into the picture of the life you are imagining. You begin picturing the

Live Your Dreams

finish line, setting goals to get the football down the field one yard at a time, focusing on the first down and moving the ball slowly down the field, one down at a time.

Think about it like a football game. You do not have to run the ball down the field all at once. Just like the quarterback who has to go through or around eleven players standing in his way, you have to slowly make yardage a few yards at a time with each play, slowly moving the ball down the field. Like football, in life there are many people standing in your way. There are obstacles. You won't make it down the field in one play. You don't have to go twenty yards at a time. In football, success is moving the ball three or four yards a play. Your goal is to get control of the ball and begin to slowly move the ball down the field a few yards at a time, making progress with each play.

We try to achieve our goals and dreams with such short timelines that we face failure and consider the game lost before the first quarter. Iterative design is about changing what didn't work, re-working the plan and design. and testing the results again and again. You will keep what works, and discard what doesn't. Each iteration will be better than the one before. With each play you have a chance to make some yardage and further the ball down the field.

This is how companies evolve over time. They try something, test it and then go back to the drawing board to make revisions. They continue this process until they have a product worthy of distribution. Each iteration of the product is better than the last one. Pattern your life design this way. Each iteration of your life will be better than the previous version. You can slowly define changes and

strive to move forward in each area of your life that you are
focused on. You will slowly move closer and closer to
where you want to be in each area of your life.

Disappointment

*"Though sorrow may last through the night,
joy comes in the morning."*

Psalm 30:5

The arrows that pierce our spirit and cause us to quit early
into the race are sorrow and disappointment. We
experience difficulty. We attempt something that we don't
achieve or we experience great disappointment and it
affects us deeply. Those arrows pierce our spirit and
deflate the balloon of dreams within us. A little part of us
dies, and we stop believing in some piece of our dreams
forever. We let that disappointment and sadness define us.
We let it set us back and often we do not pick up some of
those beliefs ever again. We consider them dead.

Sometimes it is someone that has verbally or physically
abused us and we let those arrows pierce our souls and we
begin to believe what was said about us. It could have been
a parent that said that we were incapable of doing
something and we have let that define us our whole life.
We believe we are less capable than we are. We let others
define what we are capable of and we go through life
believing that we cannot achieve the life we once imagined.
Sometimes it is a boss or a job loss that cuts deep into our
self-esteem, leaving us different than we were before the
situation. Regardless of the reason, it is imperative that you
work to believe the best of yourself. Start back at the
dream journal and allow yourself to truly imagine a new
start.

Live Your Dreams

We must work to be encouragers and believers of ourselves, and not allow our own spirits to defeat us. Find encouragers to surround you. Repair your spirit. Let yourself rebound. The greatest successes always follow failures.

We feel so far from the finish line of our dreams that we believe that it isn't worth the effort any longer. We give up completely. The important thing to remember is that the race isn't over until you take your last breath. You can begin again and remold the clay in your hands. It can become something else completely. Continue to strive to move closer to the goal. Stop accepting success in one or two areas of your life and giving up on the others altogether. This will not work long term in providing full and rich life satisfaction.

Build a belief in yourself. Recapture the bold confidence you had in yourself as a child. Remember when you thought you could be anyone, do anything, and triumph over whatever you set off to conquer? Capture a piece of that confidence that you once held, be it grade school, high school, college or afterward. Perhaps you never felt that confidence because you were bullied, mistreated, or unloved.   The God that created you and gave you talent wants you to have that confidence in yourself. Begin to develop it now and map out your new dreams in your dream journal.

Building Rome

So far you have dreamed a dream, began a dream journal, defined where you want to go, and began to define action items to get you there. Just as 'Rome wasn't built in a day,' your life transformation will take more than a day. Many that start the journey give up too soon. This is a life-planning progression and you cannot give up after a short amount of time, ruling it a failure. Your transformation will take time, but you will see progression along the way. You will see progress and when you do, reward your accomplishments.

When high-rise buildings are constructed, the plans are prepared and the building process takes years to accomplish. No one expects it to be built in less than 30 days. There is an expectation of time required. Let your journey span a few years. It is more important to move the ball further down the field. This is about moving toward the life you want to live, not about the speed with which you accomplish the journey.

Your goal is to begin to design the plans, be open to making healthy changes, and begin to walk toward the life that you were born to live. You will focus on being aware of your surroundings, and consciously making decisions about how you spend your time, where you go, what you eat, how passionately you live your life, how you work, and what you do with your spare time.

This time of building is about beginning to take action. It is less about 'thinking' and more about 'doing.' We have these ideas in our heads about what we'd like to do, and we put off even the most basic of plans. Some ideas are grand, and some are simple. Whatever the plan, we simply don't 'get to it.' We don't 'DO' anything to get it done. We keep thinking that there is more time, more life, and more opportunities. We run blind, than are caught in a time and space where we suddenly realize that life isn't filling our

Live Your Dreams

cup to overflowing. We stop to realize that we haven't lived our passions, and we have left the gifts that God gave us barren and unused. We feel uncompleted and unfulfilled. Sometimes we don't feel this until a moment in our life where whatever we have filled our life with suddenly vacates for a while; we lose a relationship, we lose a job, a child turns into an adult and moves out, or some other major life event.

We can build a life full of passion and dreams regardless of our age or how much time we have left to live. I believe that God has given you gifts, dreams, and passions. They were put there for a purpose, and our goal is to find those gifts and passions and use them for His purpose.

This is a time to build. This is your time to begin a process that will follow you through all of your days. It is time to start living intentionally.

Each year, review the plan. Look at areas that you have made the least progress. You are in a building stage. You are the contractor. It is time to assess and revamp the plan. Map out a plan to architect and build the new 'city' that you will live. Make a plan for change and be patient in the journey.

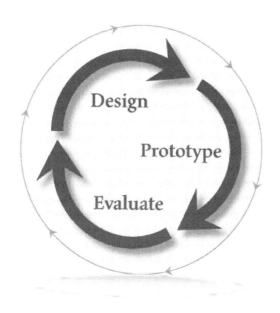

Live Your Dreams

Chapter 5 Making it Happen

"To accomplish great things, we must not only act, but also dream; not only plan, but also believe. "

Anatole France
French Poet
late 1800s

Making the Plan

In each area of your life, you will begin to construct a plan to achieve your objectives and dreams. Business executives are taught in business that 'failing to plan' is 'planning to fail.' Without a plan, things do not happen. No executive sits around his/her office and *hopes* that the things that they want their company to achieve will happen out of happenstance. Instead, they construct a plan. They put together a detailed plan that incorporates all the elements of their goals, with action items in each core area. Those action items are then turned into 'to dos' with schedules, dates, and accountability.

Nothing is left to chance. Those action items are detailed out and schedules are put in place to accomplish them. Just like in business, to accomplish your life objectives and dreams, you will start with a list of action items that, once compiled, will turn into your plan. It doesn't have to be complex. It can be a simple set of action items that you can feasibly accomplish in the next year.

Open the pages of the dream journal that you created. Circle a few of the dreams that you could conceivably start in the next year. In this journal, you envisioned the end goal, but there are preliminary goals that will get you there.

Write some action steps that you could take in the next year. Make them easy, small steps. You want to move in the direction of your dreams, yet not take on so much that you get discouraged with an inability to achieve.

Assemble the action items into a list, broken down by month. Your ability to assign these to your calendar and stick to the plan will be critical in accomplishing a forward movement to achieve your dreams.

We usually prioritize wrong. We certainly make sure that we accomplish our work responsibilities. We get the laundry done. We get the grocery shopping and chores accomplished. We take a lopsided view of life, often letting many of the important components of our life fall out of balance.

I love the television show called 'Survivor.' I find it sad when someone gets voted off after pouring so much into the game. Their chance at $1,000,000 is destroyed. In life, often we 'vote ourselves off the island.' We give up and cast aside our chances at some of the facets of our life. We don't strategize, plan or try. We just quit and leave the island. Well, in life there is a redemption island. There is a way to 'get back in the game.' It is called planning. It is about taking the dreams and passions that we have for ourselves and making action items for follow up. We then use discipline to hold ourselves accountable.

Action List

You work hard. You are dedicated. You put in the hours day after day. You rarely live your dreams. Why don't you spend more time doing what you love?

Live Your Dreams

Doing what you love and exploring your hobbies and interests is a great way to renew your mind and your body. It is a way to refresh your thoughts and energize idea generation. It is one of the best productivity tools that you possess.

After spending time on your hobbies or special interests, you work harder, approach issues with a new vigor and calmly deal with relationship stresses and strains at the office. For me, one of my hobbies is traveling.

Maybe you worry that you will lose your job if you take a vacation or live out some of your dreams, hobbies or passions. Often the opposite usually rings true. It benefits your job. You think about things differently after a break from it all. You may be able to apply something to your job that you learned reading an article or a book while you were taking time off.

The European culture embodies an expectation of taking 'holiday.' It is simply expected. Most of the people I've met while traveling abroad are from European countries or Japan, cultures that encourage time off.

Consider breaking out of your routine and taking a break from it all. I recently returned from the islands and cannot express the amazing rejuvenation and refreshed attitude that I returned with. When I'm on vacation, I spend time doing ALL the things that I love. I spend time writing, exploring, hiking, and enjoying quiet time to think. Decide to give yourself a breather. Take some time to renew your body and refresh your mind.

When you do, dream of taking regular vacations. Just like the other items in your dream journal, 'taking a dream vacation' starts with an action list. Make a simple list. Here are some ideas and action steps for a few popular areas that you may be seeking to move forward on.

Vacation Dreaming/Planning

Dreaming

Hopefully you dreamed up a few locations you'd like to visit in your dream journal. You can identify some regions

Live Your Dreams

of the world that you are interested in.   Jot down world monuments or wonders of the world that have you dreamed of seeing.   Make yourself a long list. You can use this list for the rest of your life, slowly checking off locales as you accomplish them on your life journey and adding locations as you think of new ones throughout the years.   This is just the beginning of your vacation planning action plan.

Planning

When you need a car, you sit down and plan how you will get it, what the make and model will be and then you search. It is an effort combined with plan and patience. You probably went through this same process if you are a homeowner. Traveling follows the same path. It is an effort combined with plan and patience. Different trips are available based on the budget you wish to spend and the amount of things that you decide to displace in your budget in order to travel to those locations.

The planning step can be quite fun. Technology makes it easy to download travel shows onto your handheld device, tablet, or phone; buy a travel video or use your DVR to find a travel show on a desired destination and record it. Watch the Travel Channel and use all the myriad of resources available to find locations that meet both your budget and desired type of trip: beach vacation, golf vacation, outdoors locale, Wonders of the World, national parks, family visits, etc. Talk to friends that have vacationed to various locations and get input and advice from loved ones, family, and friends.

Ask your children if there is a vacation that they have always dreamed of taking. Incorporate their dreams and aspirations into your planning process. Spend a 'date night' with your significant other planning dream vacations. This is fun to do even if you do not take the trip for several years. Dreaming and planning is fun. It allows you to go to a place in your mind that we don't often allow ourselves to go. Let yourself wander to the realm of possibilities. Enter into the 'twilight zone' of your mind, where anything is possible.

Budgeting and Saving

Several locations on your dream list now get a dollar range applied to them. To do a good job in your planning, search for some airfares and hotel costs and calculate an approximate cost for a few of the trips that bubble to the top of your 'want' list. This will help you decide how you will budget and save for the trips. Dollar ranges will also help you determine the best year for that trip based on your budget surpluses, lack of budget, or dollar amount saved.

You may decide to forego a new car, not buy that bigger house, not spend as much on clothes, and/or cancel some of your eating out trips in order to save up all year for that dream vacation. Small deviations from your expenses can create budget for travel.

Travel is a decision. If you make a decision to travel, then you must set aside resources, budget, and plan for those trips. They could be inexpensive camping trips, pricey resort destinations, or anywhere in between. The trip is about getting away, re-experiencing the joy of life, not about the cost or the destination. The trip is about living your dreams. Where have you always dreamed of going? What part of the world do you yearn to see?

Live Your Dreams

I love to travel. Because of my love for travel, I strive to forego other expenses to ensure that I have an adequate vacation travel budget. During the leaner years when the travel budgets have been smaller, I chose destinations to Asian countries that afforded a higher monetary exchange rate and allowed our money to go further. Thailand, Belize and China are good examples of inexpensive travel destinations–once you are there. Hotel and food costs are very reasonable. I actually spent less in Thailand on a two-week vacation than I did on one five-day trip to Disney World in Florida.

Make a decision to travel if that is one of your passions. Make a list of the places you'd like to go.

Categorizing

The next task is to segment your locations into budget categories. Would it take a little, a medium, or large amount of your budget dollars to get you there? Once you've done your research, you will know how to categorize the approximate cost of these dream locales. Go to www.expedia.com or American Airlines vacations and price out a few of the locations, if you have not done so. This is an important step in categorizing the potential trips. Use trip packages to give you a 'packaged price' idea. You will end up with dream destinations in three budget categories. You now have your menu of desired travel destinations sorted and categorized by price category.

Setting Aside Money

Setting aside the money for travel is next. Now that you have a vision and a menu, you can budget for the travel into bi-monthly payments where you can 'pay into' your vacation savings account. This will give you the spending money to see the world.

You could sell a second car, or take on a project in the summer that gives you extra money. You now have a place to put this extra money and a desire with how to spend it!

Scheduling/Booking

Now comes the fun part. Early in the year, you will blazingly pick dates and book your trip. You will not cancel it no matter what! There will always be something at the office or some reason to 'put it off,' but don't allow that to happen!

You will rank life and relationships higher on your priority list than your job and other distractions that will push you into cancelling. This is a priority. It is a once-a-year getaway from it all chance to rethink your priorities, re-schedule your life, and re-plan your future.

Get going, life is passing you by.

Finding the Job You Love

For some of you, vacations are not the area on which you want to focus. You want to work a job that you absolutely love. Some of you don't love your jobs. "Wow, how did this happen?" you ask yourself, again and again. You started in a job that you, well, *liked*. You worked it for a while and still liked it. Suddenly, you look up, as if from a deep slumber and you discover that you don't like your job. You could even say that you HATE your job. Good news is in store. This didn't happen overnight, and you will unfold and correct it with these simple steps.

So, the question is: **What should you do?**

Well, first of all, don't throw the baby out with the bathwater. You are thinking 'radical and extreme' change; but, is that really what you need? Start with discovering your strengths. What you LOVE and what you HATE originate from the frequency in which you are using the talents with which you were born.

Number 1: Find Your Strengths: Have you read *Now, Discover Your Strengths or The Truth About You* by Marcus Buckingham?

If not, start there.

Your end goal is to make your job incorporate as much of your strength areas as you can. When you work in your strengths, you will move toward loving your job. Your strengths will inspire you, invigorate you, and spark a fire in you!

Number 2: Market Yourself

You may hate your job because those around you don't know what you've done or what you are capable of. This is your responsibility. You are responsible to build your brand, reinforce your messaging and spread the word internally and externally about your capabilities and your strengths (once you figure out what they are). This will open up opportunities for you. Once others know what you love to do, they will recommend you for new and exciting roles and projects.

Number 3: Network

This economy is a great time to start to network if you haven't been. Begin to network with people that have jobs that you think you would love. Ask them to describe how they got into that position. Explore your possibilities.

Number 4: Make a Plan

As with all changes you dream of making, you must start with a plan and small action steps to begin moving you down the path.

This, for you, may be an area that you choose to focus. You may decide that finding a job you love is the important factor in living your 'dream life' -- that it is what has been missing in your life.

If it is, take action! Start moving in a direction that gets you in a better position. Each forward motion starts with a beginning step.

Live Your Dreams

Chapter 6 What's Holding You Back?

"The size of your success is measured by the strength of your desire; the size of your dream; and how you handle disappointment along the way."

Robert Kiyosaki
Motivational Speaker&
Author

The Chains that Bind You

There are a million reasons that you don't do what you want to do. You are held back because you are fearful of risking finances, risking love, risking anything at all. You may be too tired and worn out to do any personal planning because just getting through the day wears you out. You may be depressed and unhappy with where you are, and that feeling keeps you from making a plan to go anywhere else or do anything about it.

When you begin using the gifts that you were born with, you will be energized. If you can start to do the things you love, you will not be tired and worn out most of the time. It will improve your mood. It will slowly lift you out of the doldrums of unhappiness and move you toward a life filled with satisfaction and happiness. It is a slow gravitational pull utilizing the magnets that will move you toward a life that you are dreaming of.

What is holding you back? What is keeping you from reaching out and grabbing the dreams that are before you? Many of us just can't find the inspiration. We don't realize how short life is and we are not grabbing for our hopes and dreams. If you know of a job you've always wanted, have you applied for it? If you don't like your appearance, have you ever looked into getting a makeover or hiring a personal trainer for a period of time to get back in shape?

Why are you letting chains bind you and keep you from living the life you are dreaming of? Why are you sitting at the light, stalled, or idle?

The Quick Action Plan

As a rule, we are hesitant to spend the money, reticent to make the plan, and tardy in our actions. We continue to live a life of quiet desperation. We sometimes wonder why we can't live the life we are dreaming of; or, we don't think about it at all because thinking about it would depress us. We think of life as an endless gift, with unlimited days rather than recognizing that the clock is ticking and our time on earth is limited.

If you knew that you had a limited amount of time to live, what would you do? (Because you do have a limited amount of time to live.) You just potentially haven't focused on it. Life, from a 'limited time' perspective seems depressing. You don't focus on the short time you have, and therefore, by living in a Pollyanna world that never ends, you can't wake yourselves up into the reality that time is limited and your lack of a plan could very well result in a life barely lived.

Why not make the plan? Why not reach for the goal to get you where you want to be? Your life clock is ticking…tick tock, tick tock, tick tock, tick tock. You know what you are

Live Your Dreams

longing for. You can make a list of the things that you wish were in your life. But you haven't yet made a plan. Stop thinking about creating a life plan and start thinking about creating a six-month plan.

This is about creating a plan for the next six months. After that six-month period is up, you will make another six-month plan, and so forth. These life plans will slowly shift your focus to accomplishing the goals and aspirations in your life by focusing you on the goals, and tactical points to accomplish those goals in the short run.

These plans will break down into small, logical steps toward the direction that you'd like your life to go. Combining those steps will move you on the path toward the life of your dreams.

We make plans at work and at home all the time. We map out the goals that we must achieve and we plan out the steps to get us there. We do that with the grocery list, planning for a child going off to college, a project at work, buying a new car, etc. We know how to make a list and develop a plan; but we just don't do that in regards to our life.

We know we have to plan. Sometimes we do it innately. In fact, in some areas of life, we no longer think about it – we just do it.

Do this for your life plan. Make a six-month plan. Pick a couple of areas that you desperately want to change in your life. Pick the ones that are furthest away from where you'd like to be. Put together a simple, easy, tactical plan that gets you from point A to point B in a short amount of time. Make the goal achievable and very simple.

When I wanted to lose fifty pounds, I challenged myself to lose five pounds in two months. When you make small plans in short periods and you achieve them, you are then invigorated to strive further and press harder toward the next goal. When the goals are too hard to achieve, and you continually fail, you will find yourself giving up easily. Slow progress, over many months, is a very good way to achieve a large goal.

Success to Catapult you Forward

When you achieve a small goal, it inspires you. If your goal is a vacation yet you cannot afford a vacation, schedule an economical camping trip. Establish a tactical step toward your goal. Put something down on the calendar and do it. Take the trip in the next six months. While you are on that trip think about the next trip that you'd like to take and how you could save money toward that trip. Think of the bi-monthly costs and what it would take to go on that vacation. Slowly move yourself closer and closer to your dreams by edging your mind and your footsteps toward the goal one step at a time.

Small steps moving in the right direction will dramatically change where you are in life. Slow and steady wins the race. We give up. We give up too easily. We try something, it doesn't go as planned, and we throw in the towel. We can't do that at work, we have to get that paycheck. We can't do that at home, the house must be cleaned and the food purchased and cooked.

Live Your Dreams

We cannot do that in our personal goal setting and activation life. In the 'live the life you are dreaming of' life, you do not give up even if you have a small or large setback. You get back on the horse and keep riding toward the sunset.

Go Ahead - Spend the Time, Energy & Money

We don't afford ourselves the money, resources, time and effort toward a focused attention on living the life we were born to live. Housewives refuse to focus on themselves, they pour all their energy into the children. Businessmen/women pour all of their energy and focus into the work at the office. We lose balance and focus and before we know it, we've lost our job or moved to a different job and the children are moved out of the house.

What did we really gain by our lack of attention in our personal lives? Didn't we teach our family, spouse, children, and all those around us to do the same thing? Didn't we turn our children out into the world to live life like machines, churning out work and missing nature, love, friendships, adequate time for relationships and a relationship with God?

In doing so, we lose ourselves, and become zombies walking the earth, not living a life that excites us or keeps us invigorated or engaged. If you put a little focus on living the passions that are a part of you, you will be so much more focused and engaged for all the other areas of your life. Every area benefits from the discovery of you and what makes you tick. As you move toward living the life you were born to live, each area of your life gets a

83

bonus along the way. They get a more energized, happier, more engaged person that knows their purpose in life and enjoys living every day of the life God has given them.

You will be on fire for doing things for others. Sacrificing oneself does not enable you to pour all of your love, energy, and focus toward others; it only leaves you void and unable to love others the way that you should. Taking care of yourself and focusing on your passions is not a selfish endeavor.

You will now be able to positively impact and inspire everyone around you to do the same. You will inspire your children to live a passion-filled energized life. You will inspire your co-workers and your spouse to live the life they are dreaming of. You can become a catalyst that ignites the flames of passion for all those around you, as well as anyone that touches your path along the way. And passion is good, because life sometimes hurts and needs a healing touch.

Experiencing Failure

When you've experienced failure, your soul lands in the doldrums and you feel the sting of disappointment. You cannot imagine how this could have happened to you.

Some of the best successes in the world have followed the biggest failures. Our failures pave the road to success. We learn more, grow more, and refine our character more when we fail. The bigger we fail, the more we learn. You won't make that mistake again! It is an educational journey. It is like getting a certificate for a course completion. You've earned an education in failure. You've learned more about

Live Your Dreams

creating success from that failure than any class that you could have taken.

What do you think of when you hear the name Abraham Lincoln? Do you visualize an amazing president? Or a failed businessman? He lost an election for state legislature, and at one point had a nervous breakdown. He failed as a farmer. He was finally elected to the legislature and he lost the vote to be Speaker. He ran for Congress and lost. He ran for the U.S. Senate and lost. He even ran for Vice President and lost. He learned from his failures. He didn't think that he was somehow less of a man because of his failures. He didn't then convince himself that those failures defined him. He didn't think that now, having failed so many times, that there was no way he could lead the entire country. No, he didn't. He didn't let his failures mark him a failure.

Are your failures blurring your vision? You can still be great. Stay focused on results and the goals that spell results. Normally, you get careless and stop doing the things that you know you have to do to succeed. You start to spend more time listening to the noise around you and you are captivated by the constant movement of life.

You must continue to do the right things, go through the right motions, and side-step the thoughts and activities that are drawing you away from your coming success.

Keep getting up. Success and happiness lies in your ability to keep getting up over and over again. Everyone gets knocked down. They rarely talk about it. You are not alone. You are not the only one that has been knocked down. Keep trying. Don't take yourself down for the count. Life is about how many times you get up, not how many times you've been knocked down.

Pick yourself up, brush yourself off, and head in the direction of your passions. It doesn't matter that you've failed. It doesn't matter that you've had a setback. You cannot give up trying, you cannot give up searching. You cannot give up. Period.

Your success could be just around the corner. Brush yourself off, and go dream a new plan.

Dream a Better Dream

I love AT&T's slogan, *Rethink possible*. Isn't that what we all need to do? Don't we forget what is really possible? Don't we lower our standards and expectations of ourselves and lower the bar so that we can easily pass it?

Rethink the possible. Envision a better reality and a better future for yourself. Create a new possible. Form a new reality going forward that is all that you want it to be and then create that reality. It is easy to be pulled down into the negativity of your environment and settle for the way it is. It doesn't have to be the way it is. You control and create your possible. You create your reality.

This book is about your life. It is about rethinking your possible and adding elements that you'd like to see in your life and your schedule and creating the plan that incorporates those things into your days. Re-imagine your attitude and re-focus your energy on the positive. Re-create a new perspective and find a new joy. Realize that you can definitely have the life you are dreaming of. It will take a

Live Your Dreams

daring and bold confidence and perseverance. Today you will face the world with a new you. You will find your confidence and rethink your possible and go after it.

The stories I hear are daunting. Relationships that are dead, lives lived in virtual unhappiness, people unsatisfied with life, work, relationships, health, etc. You have convinced yourself that this is the best that it can be, but it isn't 'best' at all—it is horrible. Why accept this? It can really change. You are the only person in your life that believes that it cannot change.

Once, while sitting on the couch with the kids, I zoned into the television for a moment from my daydreaming. 'Shark Boy and Lava Girl' was on. In the movie, the main character asked what to do when your dreams are in shambles and all doesn't turn out the way that you have hoped. Lava Girl answers, "Dream a better dream."

I encounter too many people on a regular basis that have stopped dreaming. It is unfortunate. You don't have to wait until your kids are grown or you are retired to start dreaming. It is a healthy and smart tool that should be a part of your everyday life.

Dream a dream for yourself that gets you into a position, lifestyle, place or occupation that you want to be in. If your dreams have disappointed you and you feel like you are drowning in the shambles of your life, dream a better dream. Start over. Women die at the hands of their abusers because they cannot believe that they are capable of starting over. They don't believe that they are worthy of love, worthy of a great relationship, and worthy of a new start. People dragged into the sex trades believe that they are not worthy of a better plan, that life cannot be made over. They believe that their past is irrevocable.

But, it *is* erasable. It *can* be made into something new. Life can *begin* with a new plan from any point of the journey. Life can begin *today*, right now, right here as you read the words on this page.

Why go another day without a plan? Why not push forward with a new model and a new plan? You have nothing to lose. You will meet success in some areas that you target. Trying in all areas will yield success in some. Life will be better than when you started. You cannot give up. You must stay the course. It will all be worth it in the end.

Live Your Dreams

Chapter 7 Pinpointing the Action Steps

"Do you want to know who you are? Don't ask. Act!
Action will delineate and define you."
Thomas Jefferson
Founding Father

The way to get from point A to point B of your journey is to pinpoint the action steps. These steps, when scheduled and combined together with activity will move you in the direction that you want to go.

A path is best followed by putting one foot in front of the other. By this point of the book, you've accepted that you must dream, you've dreamed a new dream for your life, and you have accepted, I hope, the truth that you do control your destiny and your future. You accept that a new path is possible and now you must pinpoint the action steps, plot them on your calendar, and make things happen.

What steps would you need to take to move you forward? Remember to keep the steps simple to ensure success. Making the activities too complex or difficult will simply cause you to procrastinate. You will feel inspired if you can start defining these action steps and consider ways to begin taking the first step in each area.

Action Steps

Look back through your dream journal. Identify the pages that you rated lower than others, the ones that you had the furthest to go to reach where you wanted to be.

At the bottom of the dream journal, write a list of action steps that could start you down the path toward those dreams. Make them simple. Create consecutive steps and actions that can become points plotted on your calendar to start the journey.

You need only to come up with the beginning action steps. Each year of your annual review process, you can make additional steps to plot out for the next year. Your goal at this point is to identify the action steps for the beginning of the journey. That beginning of the journey will then be the building blocks for the next step after that.

Next to each action step, identify a time interval before the next step. Pick a month to start the process. If you have necessary activities in all six areas of your life, then you may want to space out the action steps so as not to try to do it all at one time. You are not running a marathon. You are in a life process that is more about the results than how fast you get to the next step. It is more important that the actions that you put in place are sustainable.
If you are revising your diet to become a healthier you, then put in place healthy eating habits and activities that you can sustain forever, not a fad diet and over-active workout schedule that is not sustainable. Work on coming up with action steps that you will continue for the rest of your life, not a short term-only plan that docsn't alter the life course permanently.

Live Your Dreams

You are looking to make changes that will, over time, get you into the life you are dreaming of. That new life is about altering the course, not taking an exit ramp for a quick break and then getting back on the same highway going in the same direction. That is usually how we look at these changes. You must instead consider taking a back road—a detour of sorts. You will not be getting back on the same highway. You will be re-routing your GPS to a different location, taking different roads, and changing the path and the destination.

This is not only a new route, but if your action steps begin and you follow them, you will then be not only on a new route, but you will be driving a new car that is your healthier body and ultimately a healthier you.

An example of a simple step, for instance, for weight loss, may be to remove one item from your diet this month. It may be replacing white bread with wheat bread, or replacing whole milk with two percent milk. These slow changes, added up over time, will make a difference that will positively move you in the right direction. Remember, your goal is not how fast you arrive, and how rushed you are to the finish line, your goal is to slowly make sustainable changes that will get you to your goals over time.

These action steps now need to be plotted on your calendar. If you've always wanted to volunteer for a particular organization, then put an item on your calendar to go apply for a volunteer position. Pick a random date in the future, on a day you normally don't work or after your work hours.

The month after that, you may plot an appointment to call back and check on the volunteer application.

Have a goal to improve relationships? Your action items may include a meal once a month with a friend. Pick some dates and plot them on your calendar. Pick a date to call and extend some invitations.

If your action steps are a list of activities that are too long, you must figure out a way to cut the list down to a manageable size.

Take your long list of 'to dos' and segment it into days and potential time elements. If you can whittle down your list to a conquerable size, is will be easier to accomplish. This isn't about creating another 'to do' list. This is about plotting tasks on your calendar and getting to them when you arrive at that day on the schedule. You won't see it as a list of activities; rather, you will see calendar entries merged into your year.

You will motivate yourself to achieve these action steps by creating calendar activities and small steps that you slowly achieve throughout the year.

Schedule Your Life Away

This is the time to schedule your life away. Begin translating the action items from the bottom of your dream journal into appointments in your electronic or paper calendar. Schedule out the activities for the entire year.

Schedule vacation time, family time, schedule activities you'd like to participate in, schedule planning time to plan

Live Your Dreams

activities, and book out personal time that you will define at a later point.

Begin to plot out the steps and schedule them that will move you closer to the life you are dreaming of. Think of it like a Jello mold. If you place Jello in a dish and let it harden, then you will find that you cannot add ingredients to the Jello after it hardens. The Jello is like your work. If you fill your schedule with work or kids and let it harden, it is then impossible to try to squeeze 'life' in around the hardened Jello.

If you put your personal activities into your schedule first, then let your work or kids fill the remainder of your schedule. It is like adding fruit into the mold before you add the Jello. The Jello will fill in and around the fruit and every remaining facet of the bowl, but you have already filled in your vacations, your free time, your date nights, your kid's birthdays, your anniversary, that professional basketball game you want to attend, fight night, or any other event you'd like to schedule.
If you don't know the exact date/time of the professional sporting event, reserve a spot on your calendar to check out the schedule and book the event.

Your goal is to apply action steps and schedule time on your calendar to ensure that you are, in fact, spending your time the way that you truly want to spend it.

Living the life you are dreaming of is about taking a little risk. You will move forward, walking through the doors that lead to the life you want to live. Accept that you can and will live life by doing the activities that you have scheduled. Realize that you must prioritize life and your priorities ahead of work or whatever it is that you have let get in the way of life and life balance.

Once you've scheduled the activities that are your priorities, it is very important that you follow through on each and every appointment as if your life depended upon it. You must value those appointments and keep them. They are the real priorities in your life. They are the things that will most matter 20 or 30 years from now. The other appointments on your calendar or commitments that you have may seem more important at the time, but they will not fulfill you and will not replace life balance and satisfaction.

Plot the action steps, put them on your calendar, and keep them. Make sure that you have defined the footsteps to start your path and that you have created a plan of action that you can start marching toward.

Live Your Dreams

Chapter 8: Celebrating Accomplishments & Perspective

"Stuff your eyes with wonder, live as if you'd drop dead in ten seconds. See the world. It's more fantastic than any dream made or paid for in factories. "
Ray Bradbury
American author

The best part of a life well lived is to count the many blessings and celebrate the accomplishments that you have achieved in your life. Have you attained, reached new heights, and forgot to stop and soak in the sunlight of the journey? Are you running through life so fast that you are forgetting to yell, shout, and dance for the great things in your life that you have lived through, accomplished, and participated in? Well, that can stop now.

One way to be more successful in life is to learn to be thankful for the many gifts that you have been blessed with. Work on establishing a heart of thankfulness and appreciation that can begin to form the basis for a life of joy and satisfaction.

For each slight accomplishment give yourself a reward. Commend yourself.   Celebrate the successes you and each of your family members achieve, regardless of how small they are.   Our family likes to plan celebrations for upcoming vacations by cooking special dinners highlighting the food of the country or area of the country that we will be visiting. We talk about regional foods and celebrate upcoming trips (even if the children are not attending the vacation). We plan special dinner celebrations for the family when I have closed a big deal at work or we have overcome big obstacles in our lives.

Even though two of my children are now adults and living on their own, they still regularly attend our celebratory dinners.   We still celebrate birthdays and big events as a family, gathering together and giving thanks for the blessing in our life.

You can jointly learn to celebrate life by planning events around illnesses conquered and relationships repaired. Celebrating small accomplishments will help you recognize what you've achieved and point your focus towards the positive, learning in the process to become more appreciative and thankful for the good things in your life.

Our kids come up with these phrases that make us stop in our tracks and say, "what?" One of my kid's favorite phrase is 'Go Big or Go Home'. This is a great phrase for us to take to heart. Wouldn't you have to admit that you are spending too much time on work and/or task oriented things? When it comes to celebrating your accomplishments, are you doing it half-heartedly?

Give your celebrations in life all of your attention and focused planning.   Create memorable celebrations that will become life long memories.   Work hard to create 'out of this world' type fun celebrations to make sure that you and the family remembers key life events.   Learn to celebrate your accomplishments with wanton abandon. If they aren't spectacular, shame on you! Go big or go home. Make an effort to begin grandiose celebrations that are memorable and stick with you for life.

Live Your Dreams

Everything You Need

Part of living the life you're dreaming of is establishing that you probably already have many of your needs met. The clothes that you have are good at covering your body. Your house and furnishings are probably doing a great job of covering your head and providing a good place for you to sit and to sleep, and if not, then you can work on that need. Sometimes, though, we are reaching for far too many things. Are you in desperate search for more than you need? Are you exasperating yourself in the frantic search for MORE than you need?

In a desperate search for more than you need, you begin to stress over achieving and *having stuff* supersedes your basic needs and removes the peace and satisfaction from your life. If you can accept that you may have much of what you need, it can free you up to pursue a life-long desire that is truly in your heart. We spend time searching for things that we don't need and we try to achieve more than we need to achieve.

Stop for a moment and enjoy the here and now. Stop to enjoy this moment. Enjoy the blessing that you are surrounded with. Take a moment to de-stress and take in all that you have and all that you can be thankful for. You will find that this is an important step in living the life you are dreaming of.

Perspective

Your life and the satisfaction with your life can irrevocably change for the positive if you can tap into the power of perspective.

It is not hocus-pocus. The reality is that perspective, attitude and the ability to find solutions in a myriad of problems can positively impact your life and your satisfaction with it.

You get over wrought. You get stressed out. You look at your life and see the impossibilities rather than the possibilities. You find it easier to locate the limitations when it would be more valuable to your life to find the opportunities. They are waiting for you to identify them. You may be the biggest barrier to living the life of your dreams. If you can only see the obstacles and not the path forward, then you have lost perspective and are standing in your own way.

You can easily let situations and circumstances drive you into a bitter and unhappy hole. Dig yourself out. You can become an obstacle to your own life progression if you are spending more time talking about the issues rather than focusing on the plan and the action steps to dig your way out. I am very familiar with this condition as I have lots of time right here on this step. I have wallowed in my circumstances, thrown pity parties for myself, and complained over what is missing in my life. All of these actions got me no-where but unhappy.

Turn your unhappy-with-life perspective around. This lesson is easier to conquer when you've traveled to Third World countries. After witnessing large numbers of people dying of curable illnesses that they can't afford to treat (sometimes the treatment cost less than one dollar), and meeting hundreds of children on the verge of starvation,

Live Your Dreams

one can much easier realize that you are blessed beyond belief. You can find perspective in any circumstance.

Find your true North and point your perspective and attitude in a positive place. It will benefit and bless not only yourself, but also those around you.

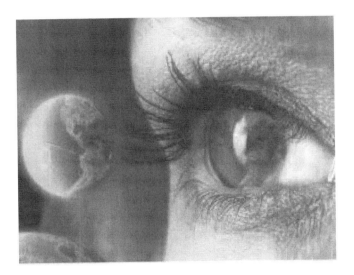

Chapter 9 Recognizing Phases and Opportunities for the New 'Go'!

"We all have possibilities we don't know about. We can do things we don't even dream we can do."

Dale Carnegie
American writer & lecturer

Life's Phases

Life is a string of phases and changes. Strung together, it forms the fabric of our lives. Each phase of our life affords us varying freedoms and desires. We don't always evaluate our life plans with regards to these phases in life that we experience. There will be better phases in your life for some of the dreams that you have. Once the children are grown and move out, you will have more freedom to live some of your dreams.

With increased freedom and less responsibilities of a high school-aged child, you may be able to begin a hobby that you've had on hold.

We get bogged down, we settle in, and we stop thinking about possible 'other realities.' It is time to evaluate your opportunities for a new 'go.' There are periods and episodes of your life that afford you the opportunity to restart. You move out of your parent's house, you graduate college, you get married, children reach a certain age or stage, you get a divorce, your husband or wife dies, you retire, etc. These life changes are a great on-ramp to start your dreaming process and activate a new plan. Keep this

Live Your Dreams

book and re-read it after each major life change. The words will have different meanings and new opportunities will arise as your life picture changes.

With each life change, you will have the chance to start a new dream and imagine a new reality for your life. Even a job loss can create an opportunity to re-evaluate the sector you work in and the type of work that you do. It can even open up opportunities to move to a new city and explore a new area of the country. Why not? What is holding you back?

The Fear of the Unknown

Often the reason that you do not grab these opportunities and run with them is a petrified fear of the unknown. You are stuck. You get stuck in cement boots that do not let you move in any direction. Fear immobilizes you and keeps you from stepping forward into an opportunity for a new life.

The unknown seems scary. It is not in your comfort zone. This is one of the most frequently encountered reasons I hear for why you are not acting on your dreams. You are scared of the unknown. You don't make a move forward in fear that moving forward will somehow land you three steps behind where you are today.

By not knowing exactly what these plans you are making will lead to, you lay in fear and do nothing, comfortable in the known and familiar. You ease your frustration by not focusing your thoughts or attention on the areas of your life that frustrate you. You refuse to acknowledge that, perhaps, doing something would be much better than doing nothing at all.

This section was created after I coached a very bright twenty-five year old in Louisville, Kentucky. He is college educated, extremely bright, and gifted in leadership. He is passionate about fitness and excellent in sales. He has been ranked as the top salesman selling fitness training packages for a prominent fitness company. He wants to do more than what he is doing today. He is not running after opportunities and seeking them out because he is afraid of the unknown. He is fearful of failure, and that fear is keeping him from progressing toward a better future. He has everything going for him, yet fear is holding him right where he is. In order to achieve and move forward, he will have to take a leap of faith and blindly trust that a movement in another direction will not cause an apocalypse in his life. Sometimes it is hard to believe in yourself if others have not boldly believed in you. If you are at this point, what can you do?

Break through your fears by writing them down. What do you think could happen? What are you afraid of? Write down your fears in detail. On paper, do they look as bad as you are making them out to be? If you believe in yourself and your capabilities, couldn't you avoid most of those listed on the paper? Couldn't you easily move back to a prior job or situation? So are you truly risking much by trying to do something different?

Fear could be keeping you from living the life of your dreams. It could be stopping you from discovering a full and rich life. It could be paralyzing you, keeping you from the love of your life, the best job you've ever worked, the

Live Your Dreams

best city you've ever lived in, or the most amazing experiences you've ever had.

Are you willing to risk that? Are you willing to walk away from some of your dreams simply because you are afraid of failure, or worse, you are afraid of success?

What if I told you that moving forward always teaches you something? Moving ahead is always a good thing. Even if you discover that it isn't what you thought it would be, you find a new experience, learn something new, and discover new people and relationships along the way. It is never a total loss. Even your failures will bring you new experiences and fun new adventures.

Take the adventure that is your life. Fill it with full and rich discoveries. Explore options and follow your dreams. Take risks and venture out beyond your comfort zone. You are writing the best story ever told: the story of your life. A good story has turns in the story line. It has romance, and drama, and family and relationships.

A good story has adventure and travel. It has bends in the story. It keeps you wondering and on the edge of your seat. You read it with anticipation. Where is the story going? Where is the story of your life taking you? Follow a path to your passions. Write a story worth telling. Write a story that takes you to the places that you want to go and builds you a path to a future that you are proud to call your own.

You can control the fear. You can paint the picture of your life. You can take the scary first few steps and start walking toward the dreams that you're dreaming.

Bethany A. Williams

Nothing ever stops you from returning to a previous position or post. Going back to a prior state is easy. Don't fear that you cannot get back to where you are. Instead, march forward to your desired destination. You can achieve your dreams.

Finding a New Start

Maybe you don't believe that you can have a new start. You can. You have to believe that it is not only possible, but likely. Understand that if you create a plan and action steps to get you there, it is definitely possible. Your new life is waiting for you. You deserve to have it. You are worthy of love, worthy of a fantastic job, and worthy of all of your hopes and dreams. You are worth more than the bad _____(fill in the blank) that you are stuck in.

It is time to find a new beginning. Take the dream journal that you created and meditate on it. Stare at the pages of it and think about the possibilities. Believe in the pages of your dreams. They are not only possible, but likely with a plan and with the action steps that you have identified.

Like a blank sheet of paper, if you apply paint and color, it will become a beautiful picture; so will the life that you are creating. The action steps and the plan is the paint and your belief in it combines to make it all possible.

Combine the action steps with perseverance and a bold belief in yourself and you will find the winning combination. Accept that you deserve this new reality. Accept the chance to start again. Many live their lives in desperation, not believing that it can be any better. Years

Live Your Dreams

go by and you become used to accepting the status quo. Instead of accepting the status quo, accept that it is time for a new start in the areas of your life that you have graded low on the satisfaction scale.

A new start can happen any day, and in any year of your life. From age 11 to age 99, at any age you can start a new plan and find a new beginning. Whether this is the beginning of your planning process post high school or college or you are retired and starting to plan for the remaining years, it makes no difference. Your new start is waiting for you today.

You look in the mirror and you don't see the possibilities. You don't see where this life can take you. You harshly judge yourself and don't see the full potential of your capabilities. Stretch your thinking. Expound on thinking that creates a resounding belief within your heart that this new start is possible.

Part of finding a new start is having a little amnesia. You must forget your failures; forget the many times you tried something that didn't succeed; and, you must, most of all, forget that you might not believe that you deserve a new start or that a new start is possible. A new start *is* possible.

Eradicate unhealthy self-talk and start affirming your decisions and ideas for new possibilities. Negative self-talk could be keeping you from living your dreams. It is time to start anew and create big, hairy, audacious goals and dreams that you strive for and believe are possible. It is time to believe that there is a genie in the bottle and you have been granted an unlimited number of free wishes.

Those wishes can and will come true and you need only to believe and strike out with purpose. It can happen if you can make your feet go in the direction of your dreams.

I have several of these big, hairy, audacious goals. I'm running toward them with wanton abandon. I will not give up. I will continue to believe that they are possible.

A new 'go' is about following the dreams that you've created with the action steps that you've defined. Work to truly believe those dreams are possible, and take the steps necessary. For example, if you believed that you were getting a new job, you would begin thinking about your first ninety days, buy some appropriate clothing, and begin planning for life post attainment of the new job. Take the steps necessary and begin walking in the direction of your dreams.

These steps will then create the beginning of your new 'go.' They will march you further down the road and, as you walk, more of the path will appear. You will be surprised as the path takes shape and maybe even stunned as you begin to arrive at the destination of some of your dreams.

Supposedly, the definition of insanity is "doing the same thing over and over and expecting different results." If that is the case, I imagine that we all live a bit in the insanity of our own lives. We continue to do the same things and *expect* a new and different life to emerge. Instead, start doing something different and *watch* a new and different life emerge.

Live Your Dreams

Start something new. Take those action steps that you outlined and do them. Force yourself into a new day and a new route. At the other end of this plan is a more content you. You will be glad that you risked it.

Each year as you revise your plan, the steps will begin to move you closer and closer to your desired destination. You will forget what it was like at the beginning of the path, for the path will have taken on such a new shape that the beginning of it will be unrecognizable.

Trust in yourself and your ability to see the other side. Trust in the God that made you to help you achieve this new start. Stop limiting His capabilities to work through you to arrive at a new destination. Believe in a new beginning.

Chapter 10: Picturing the End Result

"Finally, brothers, whatever is true, whatever is noble, whatever is right, whatever is pure, whatever is lovely, whatever is admirable--if anything is excellent or praiseworthy--think about such things."

Philippians 4:8

Now we will look at the best way to achieve success; we will picture the end result. There is something about picturing the end result that is amazingly satisfying and helpful in achieving your dreams. Whatever it takes to picture yourself in the dream, that is what you must do.

Cut out pictures of things that resemble your dreams. If it is a house you dream of, cut out a picture of a house. Put it in your dream journal. Cut out a picture of yourself and place the picture of you in front of your dream home. Cut out a picture of the island you'd love to visit. Picture success for you and imagine what that success looks like. What would an average day look like in the 'new you' world?

You have to see it, feel it, taste it and be able to touch it to truly begin to believe that it's a reality. You are 'selling' the story to your heart and mind. You must convince your subconscious mind. You are convincing the 'you' inside that you really believe in this new path. Over time, you will gain the ability to picture it. You will see the path before you more clearly. You will begin to set out a path to follow that you can see. The light will appear at the end of a long tunnel. Instead of feeling blind, you will feel like

Live Your Dreams

someone has put glasses on you. You will use laser focus to visualize your dreams and the new reality that will become your future life. It is as if you can visualize traveling in a time machine and landing in the future. You can see what that future could look like.

Always hope for the best. Always continue believing that your reality can change for the better. Continue to plot points and action steps. Continue to annually set your goals and expectations. Keep working toward achieving the passions in your heart. Don't give up. The journey is worth it.

It is a bit like saving money. If you put away six dollars and fifty cents a day, it doesn't seem like much really. But if you take that money, saved for twenty years, compounded monthly at six and a half percent and you would have over a million dollars at the end of that twenty years. (Wow, that's hard to believe that with $6.50 a day for 20 years, you could have a million dollars in savings.) Your life plan is like that. By making calculated simple steps and following an action plan, you will slowly achieve the dreams that are bursting to break out of your inner self.

We spend so much time in the present and our crash into reality that it is often hard to envision it a different way. It is hard to picture a varying reality when all we can see is where we are today. If we want to lose weight, it is hard to picture success because every mirror that we pass shows us an image of that we look like now. So cover all the mirrors and focus on the numbers on the scale and a really healthy diet and exercise routine.

I'm referencing an action plan, like discussed in Chapter 7, that entails simple and easy steps in the right direction. Maybe you start with ten minutes of walking a day. Simple easy steps compounded over time that slowly involve more and more effort as you attain success and realize that the planning process combined with simple action steps really works.

Take all your energy and efforts and picture your new future. Picturing success is a critical component. You have to believe it and be able to picture it. We are so accustomed to the way things are today that we can't always stretch our thinking and believe that things can change.

You work a job you hate, for example, and put in ridiculous hours and punish yourself year after year with the job. Like putting up with an abusive relationship, you put up with a job that is abusing your time, sucking the life out of you, and shifting your valuable priorities. You can't imagine that you will be able to find another job with better characteristics for the same pay, so you do not look for another job with your whole heart and you live in discontent and dissatisfaction of your current situation. Picture the end result. Now, believe that you can find a better job with better hours and characteristics. This is a critical part of the process. You cannot live your dreams until you can convince yourself that you can, really, live your dreams.

I meet with people crying out for a change in an area of their life. They want it to change. They tell me that they desperately want a change. They are half-heartedly seeking change with a few actions and activities that show that they

Live Your Dreams

are marginally interested in the change that they are swearing is of utmost importance to them. Believe in this change so much that you chase after it whole heartedly, earnestly believing that it is not only possible, but that it is the most likely scenario. Run, not jog, after it. Flee your current situation and speed down the path of change as fast as your little heart can go.

Do not go hesitantly into the future. March forward confidently. If you earnestly want a change, then you must picture the end result with confidence. Believe in an alternate reality. Run toward it. Seek the future and the dreams that you want. Imagine that this alternate future is a pot of money waiting for you. You wouldn't casually walk after a box filled with a million dollars, would you? You are casually walking along toward an amazing future.

This is the chapter where you move the casual thoughts about a possible future to an earnest run toward a real prize that you know is your future. You, in your mind, must move from possibilities to the definitive destinations of your life.

Picturing More Time with the Kids

Sometimes you feel just-plain-guilty about working too much. You wonder if you've been a good enough mom or dad and worry about how the kids will turn out with you spending so much time at work.

Just like in the other areas of your life, the best way to fight working-parent guilt is to make a plan. Even moms and dads that stay at home often are so overwhelmed that they struggle to spend quality time with their children. You really can't get caught in the trap of comparisons. You have what you have today, and a plan will help you move more toward where you want to be. In this scenario, as well, you must picture the end result.

Make a plan to do the following:

- Plan one-on-one time every week with each child individually.
- Each evening, ask your children what was the best and worst parts of their day. Spend time understanding what is going on in their worlds. Each will have unique challenges and life events unfolding.
- Create 'anchor' events. These are memorable outings that create memories that they will remember for years to come. Some great examples are museums, boat rides, attending a musical or sporting event, or taking a trip.
- Enjoy 'theme night dinners' or celebrations representing other cultures or simply pick a sporting event. You could have a baseball-themed dinner with hotdogs, popcorn, and all the fixings of the ball stadium.
- Have a story time. Read a story that your child loves. Often we stop this when they are older, but I've found that even16 year-olds that like a good story now and again.
- Go outside and play catch, basketball, Frisbee, or chase. Enjoy fun physical activities together.

In order to combat working parent guilt, regularly create fun things to do with your children. Become an active part of their lives. Find ways to enjoy your time together and

Live Your Dreams

make incredible memories. Your unfailing love and acceptance is what they desperately need from you and they can certainly get that even if you have a busy schedule.

Cut yourself some slack. Picture a new future if that is what you want. If you can visualize even more time with them, then motivate yourself to find that new job, new opportunities or new city to move to. In the meantime, focus on what you can do and what you can provide. Beating yourself up mentally won't make the current situation any better. Work with what you have. Brimming with Commitments

I'm consistently intrigued by the fact that, as a general rule, the majority of the population doesn't schedule the things they enjoy doing or want to do. We continually miss scheduling the things that we really want to do in life.

I think that one reason that we don't get what we want done is because we have no margin. We leave little margin in our life for any planning, thinking, or the scheduling necessary to plan events that are a part of living the life of our dreams.

We leave no time for planning these desired events, and often don't even find time for the things that we have to do in order to get through day to day life. Accomplishing things above and beyond the normal day to day routine of life seems problematic, difficult, and – well – often just impossible.

We need to leave margin in our schedules. We need to have some unscheduled days and some 'openings' to then find time to do all the things mentioned in this book.

If you are feeling overwhelmed and unable to get to anything you'd like to do, start by clearing off your schedule and leaving some margin in your life. This will give you time to think, time to focus, and time to concentrate your activities and energies on things that you want to have in your life.

Once you have conquered this, and you begin to schedule some of your wanted activities, those activities will then charge your inner battery. Doing the things that you love will give you energy and you will find, over time, that you have more and more margin, and more and more time to schedule these activities. Living the life you're dreaming of works to fill a need inside of you and once you start down the path, the road gets straighter and easier to follow.

Go For It

Sometimes you have to just go for it. You have to run after your goals with wanton abandon. Take a flying leap and land somewhere closer to where you want to be. Quit worrying about failing. All great successes follow failures. Jump out and risk failure. Jump forward despite the potential consequences. By doing that, by taking that leap of faith and making a plan and marching forward, you will land closer to a new reality that you enjoy living in.

You may not know if it will truly get you where you want to go. But take this leap with a giant dose of faith, hoping that you will, in fact, land closer to the goal. The place you

Live Your Dreams

land will be more focused on the satisfaction and peace that life can hold for you. Go for it. Reach out and make a plan.

Put away your inhibitions and douse your fears. Stop listening to those little voices in your head that say, "This is unfair to my children," or "This is unfair to my spouse." Make a plan and start moving toward it. Encourage those around you to start doing the same. Think about this: You can create a reality where each of you is stretching forward and reaching toward the life you were born to live. If you are all stretching forward to live the life you were born to live, a life of satisfaction and excitement, wouldn't that be a great household to be living in? A great place to work? And wouldn't those be great friends to hang out with?

This would make for very exciting and interesting discussions. I challenge you to go for it. I dare you to make a plan, step forward, as simple as it may be and start marching in the direction that you want to go. The results will be dramatic.

Never Give Up

Sometimes we resign ourselves to the fact that we simply cannot have the life of our dreams. We go forward trying to live life in mediocrity, accepting life as it comes to us and believing in our hearts that this is the best that we can do, the best that it can be, and that it cannot be improved upon.

Do not accept a mediocre existence. Why would you accept the status quo and believe that it could be no better? What do you really risk if you try to change it and do not succeed? Are you not just back where you started, no worse off than now? Isn't that worth the risk?

Success doesn't come easily and you do not achieve it without a precursor of failures. In our fear of not reaching success, sometimes we avoid the steps necessary to achieve success. We read stories of successful people and often we focus only on their success, not the path that they had to take to get there. Success and determination go hand in hand. If you want it bad enough, you can achieve it.

If you are willing to put in the time, effort and energy required, you will face better odds at success. Don't be reluctant to pound the pavement. Don't be reluctant to go further, work harder, and make special efforts to stand out. You will succeed in living the life of your dreams if you are able to extend effort and not give up.

You have so much more to gain. Convince yourself that you should try. You should aim higher, set targets and try to achieve them. You will achieve some of those targets and it will shift your life into a different place than you are today.

Live Your Dreams

Chapter 11 Making it Work & Staying Focused

"The mass of men lead lives of quiet desperation..."
Henry David Thoreau

"Alas for those that never sing,
but die with their music still in them"
Oliver Wendell Holmes

As we discussed in the last chapter, in order to end up with the million dollars after saving for 20 years, you have to continue to put away the $6.50 a day. You can't give up mid-stream and still achieve the savings goal. It only works with the continuous dedication of the twenty years. It won't work unless you stay focused on the goal. The same is true of living your dreams. They need a long-standing dedicated focus from you.

Your goal is to live a life of no regrets. You want to ensure that the decisions you've made, the parts of your life you've sacrificed, the time you've spent with your family and the time you've taken to do the things you love would all be the decisions that you would agree were the rights ones were you reviewing your life years from now.

You must stay focused to live the life that leaves you satisfied. You are to live the life that measures success in your eyes, not the eyes of others. Do not succumb to a lifetime of slavery trying to live up to other people's expectations of you. You own your destiny, your future, and it is up to you to stay focused on your goals.

When you reach the end of your days, you will ask yourself, did you follow your dreams? Were you truly yourself? You can risk your fears and trepidations and take the journey of discovery to a new and better future, and that journey will be worth taking.

The Balls Will Fall

In your attempt to enjoy it all, realize that you cannot *do* it all. You cannot even brush the surface. Accept it and move forward, understanding that you are juggling a big load and sometimes, some of the balls will fall. Sometimes, your boss will be unhappy with you; sometimes your kids will be disappointed in you; and, sometimes you will not be able to get it all done well. We are too good at capturing the falling balls at work and with our chores, and less good at allowing those balls to fall so that we can ensure success in our relationships and home life.

Accept defeat in small areas to become a king or queen of prioritization. It isn't important that you get everything done; but it is critical that you get the most important things done. Why are you prioritizing the wrong falling balls?

What would you do to make sure that you didn't lose a key customer? Is it more than you would do to make sure your teenager knows you love him/her, or to save your marriage, or your relationship with your parents?

What will it take to re-prioritize the dropping balls in your life?

Live Your Dreams

Try some of these simple ideas:

- **Cross items off your list.** In the book *Good to Great*, Jim Collins tells you to take things off of your to do list. To be great, you must move toward concentrating on less things. You have to do less things better. So to start, cross off items on your list that you can give to others, hire out, or simply put off for another day, week or month the things that you do not have to do.
- **Prioritize your list by your assigned values.** Are you doing the things that you value the most? Or are you simply doing what comes natural? Make a conscious decision to prioritize the right things first. Compare your list to your value statement and prioritize it accordingly.
- **Reward your success.** Reward yourself for things you've accomplished.

Chapter 12 Living the Dream

"You've got to eat while you dream. You've got to deliver on short-range commitments, while you develop a long-range strategy and vision and implement it. Success is doing both; getting it done in the short-range and delivering a long-range plan, and executing on that."

Jack Welch
Former CEO, General Electric

The Greater Plan

It is time to go live your dreams. You were pulled toward this book for a reason. You are reading it now–at this point in your life–to spark a change. Life has no coincidences.

Life is throwing you choices, a chance and an opportunity to change your game. It is up to you to push forward with energy, ambition, and drive. Your natural tendency is going to be to stick to the status quo. You will naturally feel magnetically pulled to stay on the path that you've been on. Change can be hard. But YOU, not your habits, are in control.

Life is about choices. You are driving your life. You choose the choices and the direction that your life is taking. If you do not like the direction that you are going, then change your path.

You will now boldly move ahead, trusting in your own abilities, and knowing that where you have been brought you to this particular point in your life. You will believe

Live Your Dreams

that there is more ahead and know that you control your destiny.

Walk forward, grateful beyond belief, for where you are today and excited about where God will take you next.

Life is a Gift

Life is a gift. We unwrap it each day, savoring the gift we've been given. Your fortitude and perseverance should not waver. Stick to your path. You will experience success in some areas, and not so much success in other areas. Your goal is to enjoy and delight in the areas that you find success. Your aim is to go live the dream and make your life the best that it can possibly be.

We are surrounded by enticing television commercials and the negativity of the world that try to convince us that we are not enough, we don't have enough, and that our lives are not good enough.

You will control these external stimuli and drive your life forward by doing the things that you deem important, not the things that the world holds in high esteem. You will build a life that you can be proud to call your own.

Now you can move forward with a full understanding of where you'd like to be going. You are SVP of your life. You are committed to a lifetime of out-of-the-box idea creation to create your dream life.

Your future is a mystery. Your life is a book that you are writing and the ending is still unknown. You can be anything, go anywhere, and achieve whatever you set out to achieve. You are driving the bus that is your life. You are in control of this gift of life and the decisions that you make.

Begin writing the story that you want to live. Begin making decisions and moving yourself in the direction that you want to go. You can go places that you've never dreamed of and arrive places that you never thought you'd be.

Keep stretching, keep searching, keep pressing the limits. Stretch further, reach farther. Create goals and plans that you can run after and achieve.

In a year, ask yourself, are you living in the moments of your life? Have you dared to explore and enjoy life's twists and turns? Are you courageously enjoying your life? Do you take what life throws you and use it? What are you missing? What apparent message is staring you down that you have avoided?

Life is about choices. You get caught up in all the choosing and the most important elements of life can blur from your focus. You need to have a magnifying glass pointed at the important focal areas of your life: loved ones, health, rest, living your passions, God, and family.

It takes effort, energy, and participation to run after your dreams. I recently heard a statistic that out of work people are spending their time watching TV and sleeping in, not exercising and following educational dreams as you would hope they would be. Why is that? The battle to success and accomplishment starts in your head. You have to believe that you can get there.

Live Your Dreams

Without believing, you won't do the physical tasks
necessary to catapult you into your dreams. If you can't
believe and dream, how can you get others to believe in
you? Your beliefs and the ability to visualize yourself
succeeding is the first step to running after your dreams.

Now you are to simply put one foot in front of the other.
March toward your new life. Continue to march ahead and
design your life.

Accept this new role of designer and producer and mold
your life into what you'd like it to be.

Attitude is everything. If you can keep a positive attitude,
you will always stand out and shine. You will have a
positive outlook that rubs off on others around you and
increases your satisfaction with the life you have.

Grasp life by its tail. Live in the moment rather than barely
living. Think about your life and the precious gift that it is.

Live the life that you were born to live. I know you can.
Go do it. You can start today!

Why Do I believe that You
Can Design the Life
You Want to Live?

Because I have...

Gradually Living a Healthier Life

2003 Size 14   2004 Size 10   Now Size 6

Live Your Dreams

Weight Journey
Before:

After:

You can achieve success at any age. I am in my late
forties, yet I will continue to strive to maintain a healthy
weight and lifestyle regardless of my age.

Live Your Dreams

The Travel Journey

From a life of no travel to life with annual trips:

- **1998**
  - Jamaica
- **1999**
  - Hawaii
  - Antigua, West Indies
- **2000**
  - Niagara Falls, Canada
  - Snoqualmie Falls, Washington
- **2001**
  - Lake Tahoe, Nevada & Las Vegas
- **2002**
  - Tour of Italy
  - Paris, France
  - Scottsdale, Arizona
  - Seattle, Washington
  - Ghana, Africa Mission Trip
  - Nassau, Bahamas
- **2003**
  - Turks & Caicos Islands
  - Paris, France
- **2004**
  - Mykonos & Athens Greece & London
  - Virgin Islands
- **2005**
  - Belize, Central America
  - Aruba
- **2006**
  - Phuket & Bangkok, Thailand
  - Tokyo, Japan
  - Acapulco, Mexico
  - Denali, Alaska

Bethany A. Williams

- **2007**
  - Great Wall, China
  - Playa Del Carmen, Mexico
  - Kona, Hawaii
- **2008**
  - Dominican Republic
  - Rio de Janeiro, Brazil
- **2009**
  - St Kitts, West Indies
  - Grand Canyon
- **2010**
  - Bora Bora, French Polynesia
  - Costa Rica
- **2011**
  - Barbados
  - Las Vegas, Nevada
  - Singapore
  - Lankawi, Maylasia
- **2012**
  - Macho Picchu, Peru
  - Galapagos Islands, Ecuador
  - Paris, France
  - Tour of Italy: Venice, Florence & Rome
- **2013**
  - Kauai, Hawaii
  - Jamaica
  - San Diego
- **2014**
  - Maui, Hawaii
  - Rio de Janeiro, Brazil
  - Venice Beach, California